Praise for *The Advocate Educator's Handbook*

"The notion of 'Brave Education' is never in opposition to the idea of a 'safe education.' Safety is just such a low bar and should be an inalienable feature of public education, not optional or a bragging point. *The Advocate Educator's Handbook* supports the notion that schools have to, first, be safe enough to honor the bravery so many LGBTQ+ students and educators are already demonstrating. Schools that promote a safe and excellent education for all students need this handbook if genuinely committed to living into that promise."

—**Tim'm West**, M.Ed., Executive Director, LGBTQ Institute at the National Center for Civil and Human Rights

A resource such as this couldn't come at a more crucial time, as transgender youth in the U.S. have become the opportunistic targets of the escalating waves of anti-trans rhetoric and legislation. With its comprehensive and methodical approach to tackling challenging issues facing advocates for transgender rights, this handbook will become a fundamental tool for anybody who works with and serves youth.

—**Rodrigo Heng-Lehtinen**, Executive Director, The National Center for Transgender Equality

"For educators, administrators, school staff, and anyone else who has asked, 'How can I best support transgender students?'—this book is for you. *The Advocate Educator's Handbook* is scaffolded to meet educators where they are, and is a critical tool for creating safer, more inclusive learning environments for transgender students everywhere."

—**Keygan Miller**, Director of Public Training, The Trevor Project

"This is my job in a book! *The Advocate Educator's Handbook* is a one-stop shop for all the need-to-know information on supporting trans, non-binary, and gender-expansive youth in schools. It is an invaluable resource for educators and youth-serving professionals who want to implement equitable practices for LGBTQ+ youth."

—**Booker Marshall**, LGBTQ and Sexual Health Manager, Chicago Public Schools

"Ford and Kling have written one of the most comprehensive tools for educators not only to understand how to help LGBTQ+ thrive, but to understand how to position themselves, as educators, in the journey to understanding, acceptance, and advocacy of their students. Every teacher, counselor, administrator, and parent should know this book."

—**Willie Carver**, Author of *Gay Poems for Red States*, 2022 Kentucky Teacher of the Year, Member of the American Federation of Teachers National LGBTQ+ Task Force

"A modern guide for anyone seeking to boldly support transgender and non-binary students. Resources, reflection, real situations—all in one."

—**Levi Arithson**, Program Manager, LGBTQ+ Equity Initiatives, Denver Public Schools

"This book could not come at a more critical time. Any youth-serving professional or family member looking for tools to advocate for LGBTQ+ youth should read this book. I am grateful for the concrete strategies to ensure LGBTQ+ youth are in environments where they are valued and can be their authentic selves."

—**Cheryl Greene**, Senior Director, Welcoming Schools, Human Rights Campaign Foundation

"*The Advocate Educator's Handbook* is an accessible and comprehensive toolkit that teachers, administrators, policymakers, and parents can use to create more inclusive, affirming, and joyful educational experiences for trans and non-binary youth. By asking them to reflect on their own motivations, knowledge, and commitment to education, Ford and Kling inspire readers to disrupt inequitable policies and practices to better meet the needs of our gender-diverse students."

—**Sara Moore**, Associate Professor and Chairperson of Sociology, Salem State University

"As a parent of a trans youth, navigating the school system felt like an overwhelming and intimidating process. This book makes it less so! Every parent of a transgender kiddo should read this book and feel confident that their child can and should be supported in their schools and by their peers. Every teacher should read this to learn how to support and cultivate an inclusive classroom! This is a must read!"

—**Lizette and Jose Truillo**, Parent Advocates

"This book is a fantastic resource, and I cannot wait to share it with educators throughout Minnesota! Whether you are new to these concepts or a seasoned advocate, this book has something that each of us can learn. As states and municipalities across the country pass vastly different policies regarding transgender and nonbinary children, this book offers steps that each of us can take, within the bounds of our local laws, to support a school atmosphere that allows transgender and non-binary students to thrive. Thank you for creating such an amazing resource!"

—**Kelsey Waits**, Activist and Founder of Transparent Alliance

"A timely and much-needed handbook! EDI (Equity, Diversity, and Inclusion) practitioners, consultants, and facilitators like myself—not just teachers and school administrators—will learn and benefit greatly from reading and using this excellent guide."

—**Yee Won Chong**, Senior Racial Equity Fellow,
Western States Center for EDI

"*The Advocate Educator's Handbook* is beautifully written, clear, comprehensive, specifically helpful, warm, and open...open to human potential, to change, and to more beautiful, meaningful, joyful exchanges in our classrooms, led by, and centered on, trans joy."

—**Joji Florence**, Co-Founder of Trans formative Schools

The Advocate Educator's Handbook

The Advocate Educator's Handbook

Creating Schools Where Transgender and Non-Binary Students Thrive

Vanessa Ford, M.A.T.
and
Rebecca Kling

JB JOSSEY-BASS™
A Wiley Brand

For general information on our other products and services or for technical support, please contact our Customer Care Department within the United States at (800) 762-2974, outside the United States at (317) 572-3993 or fax (317) 572-4002.

Wiley also publishes its books in a variety of electronic formats. Some content that appears in print may not be available in electronic formats. For more information about Wiley products, visit our web site at www.wiley.com.

Library of Congress Cataloging-in-Publication Data:

Names: Ford, Vanessa, author. | Kling, Rebecca, author.
Title: The advocate educator's handbook : creating schools where
  transgender and non-binary students thrive / Vanessa Ford and Rebecca
  Kling.
Description: Hoboken, New Jersey : Jossey-Bass, [2024] | Includes index.
Identifiers: LCCN 2023043579 (print) | LCCN 2023043580 (ebook) | ISBN
  9781394178018 (paperback) | ISBN 9781394178025 (adobe pdf) | ISBN
  9781394178032 (epub)
Subjects: LCSH: Gender identity in education. | School environment. |
  Transgender students.
Classification: LCC LC212.9 .F67 2024 (print) | LCC LC212.9 (ebook) | DDC
  370.81—dc23/eng/20231024
LC record available at https://lccn.loc.gov/2023043579
LC ebook record available at https://lccn.loc.gov/2023043580

Cover Design: Wiley
Cover Images: © Alona Savchuk/Shutterstock

SKY10062102_120723

This book is dedicated to our parents,
who were our first teachers, and to trans youth
everywhere who inspire us every day.

"One child, one teacher, one book, one pen
can change the world."

—Malala Yousafzai

"I like to reassure educators: you already know
how to do this. You just need to trust that you know
how to do this."

—Kyle Lukoff

Contents

Foreword

WE CAN all agree that great teachers, without exception, have a lasting impact on the students they teach. As an educator, I am (was) in a constant state of curiosity, awareness, and appreciation of the importance and value of the experiences I had each day with students.

Relationships matter, a sense of belonging is critical, and we cannot allow discrimination to be a part of the lives of the young people we help shape.

Educators recognize and acknowledge the struggles of marginalized communities, including the LGBT+ youth. The school environment is meant to be a safe and nurturing space for students to grow, learn, and discover themselves. However, for many LGBT+ students, a school can be a challenging and even hostile environment. As educators, we are responsible for ensuring that every student, regardless of their sexual orientation, gender identity, or expression, feels supported and respected in our classrooms.

For this reason, I am excited to introduce *The Advocate Educator's Handbook: Creating Schools Where Transgender and Non-Binary Students Thrive*. Vanessa Ford and Rebecca Kling have gifted us with this brilliantly written book, a comprehensive resource for teachers looking to educate themselves on the issues faced by transgender and non-binary youth, and learn how they can create an inclusive and supportive classroom environment. This guidebook is written by experienced educators and LGBT+ advocates who have firsthand knowledge of these students' challenges and the best ways to support them.

The book provides a roadmap for teachers to understand the struggles of LGBT+ youth in schools, and offers concrete strategies to make classrooms and school environments more inclusive. The authors also discuss the importance of intersectionality, acknowledging that the struggles of LGBT+ youth intersect with other aspects of their identity, such as race, ethnicity, and ability.

The book provides insights into creating a safe and welcoming classroom space through inclusive language, diverse literature, and teaching materials. It also explores how teachers can become influential allies for transgender and non-binary students, and become an advocate for them. For teachers who may need help understanding LGBT+ identities and experiences, the guidebook offers an overview of the terminology, history, and culture of the LGBT+ community.

In addition to providing information and strategies, the guidebook also offers examples of real-life scenarios that teachers may encounter in the classroom. It provides guidance on how to handle these situations. For instance, the book explores how to support a student who has just come out, how to respond to homophobic or transphobic comments made by other students, and how to handle bullying and harassment.

I was recently touched by the words of an immigrant teacher who came to this country not speaking the language and the sense of belonging teachers provided her, "I've been able to witness the beauty of our nation from perhaps a different lens, a lens that pays special attention to those who wrap their arms around those of us who are a little bit different. Often those who held me literally and figuratively were my teachers." ~Rebekah Peterson— 2023 National Teacher of the Year

What we do and say as teachers matters! I learned even more with every page I read, and I am thankful for the opportunity to grow and put my learnings into practice.

The cruelty of ignorance, the discomfort of guilt, and intentional discrimination can be decreased and hopefully eliminated if we all do our homework!

~Peggy Brookins, NBCT
President and CEO, National Board of Professional
Teaching Standards

Author Bios

Vanessa Ford (she/her) is an award-winning educator and author. Her children's book *Calvin* won the 2022 Lambda Literary Award for Best Children's Book. Vanessa was a classroom teacher for 14 years in Washington, D.C., Public Schools, and her advocacy has been featured in the *New York Times*, *Washington Post*, *Boston Globe*, *Newsweek*, and NPR. She was a founding member of The Human Rights Campaign's Parents for Transgender Equality Council and sat for two years on the board of the National Center for Transgender Equality. She lives with her husband and two children, one of whom is trans, near Boston. Learn more about Vanessa's work at www.jrandvanessaford.com.

Rebecca Kling (she/her) is an educator, organizer, storyteller, and advocate for social change. Rebecca served as the community storytelling advocate and director of education programming at the National Center for Transgender Rights as well as on the leadership team of Harbor Camps, a sleepaway summer camp for trans and non-binary youth. She is also the co-founder of Better World Collaborative, a social impact consulting firm working to combat the recent flood of anti-trans legislation. She lives in Chicago with her two cats. Learn about Rebecca's work at www.rebeccakling.com and www.bwcollab.com.

Introduction

> "Our role [as educators] is to try to meet young people where they are and to be relevant so that when we say things, or we set up a classroom, it's actually something young people opt into with their minds and their hearts, so they are willing to say, 'I'll learn something from you.'"
>
> —Bex Mui (she/her),
> Director of Stonewall National Education Project

THIS BOOK is intended for anyone who helps shape the educational experiences of transgender and non-binary youth. (For a glossary of the terms and definitions used throughout this book—including *transgender, non-binary, gender binary,* and more—see Chapter 2.) You may be a classroom teacher, a school administrator, a policymaker, the parent of a trans student, or simply someone who wants to create safer, more inclusive, and more affirming classroom environments. You may even be trans yourself!

Using This Book

How ever you have arrived here, we encourage you to use this book in whatever way makes the most sense to you. For those at the beginning of their allyship journey, it may make sense to read the book in order from cover to cover. For folks with a little more knowledge, feel free to skip around, jump right to a particular section, or identify the potential obstacles to equality that exist in your school community and go from there. At the end of each chapter, you'll find thoughts on addressing real-world challenges and questions for personal reflection. And while these can be helpful for individual learners, we also hope they can provide some focus and structure for book groups or community learning.

With that in mind, we hope you'll use the resources in this book not only to educate yourself but to educate your peers and colleagues as well. We'd like to think that the adults in your school community want all students to learn, grow, and thrive, but it's critical to dig into whether or not those goals are actually being achieved. Melinda Mangin (she/her)—author of *Transgender Students in Elementary School* and a professor in the Department of Education Theory, Policy, and Administration in the Graduate School of Education at Rutgers University—put it this way: "Most educators are well intentioned, want to do better, and aren't trying to cause harm. That said, the best of intentions doesn't mean you aren't creating harm."

But you don't need to go it alone! We believe that if you are looking to better support trans and non-binary students, others in your school community are looking to do so as well (they just might not be very public about it). It's possible that your school or district already has resources, policies, or best practices on working with trans and non-binary students. For example, Booker Marshall (they/he), the LGBTQ+ and Sexual Health Program Manager with Chicago Public Schools, cites "the demand from schools" as the primary reason for the growth of the Chicago Public Schools resources and professional development for creating LGBTQ+ supportive environments.

Even if you have not yet found allies in your community, you don't have to go it alone because you have the advice and encouragement of everyone we consulted over the course of writing this book. We conducted more than 50 interviews, speaking with educators, advocates, and researchers as well as trans youth and their families. Those interviews all took place in late 2022 and early 2023, mostly via Zoom. Quotes from those conversations can be found throughout these pages.

And while the data, organizations, and policy conversations mentioned in this book are U.S.-focused, the best practices for working with trans and non-binary students are broadly applicable. Likewise, if the resources you want don't yet exist in your school or district, you may be the perfect person to get the ball rolling by hosting a book group, sharing excerpts with colleagues and peers, or simply bringing a new perspective to your existing work.

We also know that advocating for trans and non-binary rights can be emotionally draining. That's why we spoke with trans students about what brings them joy and what gives them hope for the future. We'll be sprinkling those throughout the book as well as some trans joy thoughts and resources we've seen elsewhere. In the Conclusion, we also have thoughts about hope for the future from trans students.

Trans Joy

The best thing [about being trans or non-binary] is being able to express who I am and not having to be limited by the gender binary. I feel complete and amazing!

—Emma (she/her), 14

Finally, while this book is mainly intended for adults, we always recommend that you work *with* trans and non-binary students, rather than simply assuming you (as the adult) know what issues are the most important to them.

Focusing on Trans and Non-Binary Students

Every student deserves a learning environment in which they can thrive as their full, authentic selves. So then, some might ask, why should we focus specifically on how to support trans and non-binary students? There are a few ways to answer this question.

Trans and Non-Binary Students Need Support

Simply put, trans and non-binary students face challenges that their cis peers do not. The Trevor Project's 2021 *National Survey on LGBTQ Youth Mental Health* found that:

- More than 3 in 4 trans and non-binary youth reported symptoms of generalized anxiety disorder in the past two weeks.

- More than 2 in 3 trans and non-binary youth reported symptoms of major depressive disorder in the past two weeks.

- More than half of trans and non-binary youth had seriously considered suicide in the past year.[1]

The Trevor Project also found that affirmation and support can be life-saving. Respecting the names and pronouns of trans and non-binary youth, and allowing them to change legal documents is associated with lower rates of attempted suicide.[2] Here's how Keygan Miller (they/them), Public Training Manager at the Trevor Project, put it:

> Students are spending a third of their day or more in schools. And so if a young person is LGBTQ, the impact on their daily life of an affirming space is hugely shaped by [their] school, especially if they don't have an affirming home life; school might be the only space for that. And we know from our research that when LGBTQ students can have access to affirming schools—and trans students have support from their teachers and peers—they have lower rates of attempting suicide, they have less mental health issues, etc.
>
> In fact, if you look at affirming spaces—schools, home, community, etc.—schools actually have one of the highest connections to lowering those rates, when [the school is] affirming. So that's a big deal. And we also know from our national survey research that when young people learn about LGBTQ people and issues in school, we also see significantly lower odds of a suicide attempt by our LGBTQ students. So just by

learning LGBTQ history, or learning about an LGBTQ
person, that can lower those [suicide] rates.

Schools then become this twofold space: What
are we learning about, how are we growing in our
understanding of our community? But also, where
can I find that safe and affirming space? You have to
be addressing both of those pieces. And doing that is
going to increase [student] mental health and lower
suicidality.

Ultimately, increased visibility of trans people across the
United States has resulted in both greater support and greater
pushback. One 2022 survey found that, paradoxically, more and
more people in the United States favor protecting transgender
people from the abstract idea of "discrimination," but also that
more and more people believe gender is solely determined by
someone's sex at birth.[3] (See the Glossary of Terms and Definitions
in Chapter 2 for more on what that "sex assigned at birth" means,
and why this survey presents something of a paradox for trans
people.) Trans and non-binary students need focused attention to
ensure that vague or generalized ideas of support are translated
into actual policy and practice.

Logan Casey (he/him), Senior Policy Researcher & Advisor
for the Movement Advancement Project (MAP), told us about the
double-edged sword of visibility:

While knowing a trans person doesn't magically fix
everything, it does—for a lot of people—really help
begin a journey of changing hearts and minds. But
it's a double-edged sword: growing visibility is good
because it helps us as trans people find each other, and
not having to grow up the way I did, for example,
with not knowing any trans person, or even what a
trans person was, other than these really awful carica-
tures in the media that often ended in violent ways.
There are some good things about that growing visibility, what it means for us as a trans community, and
being able to find and see and connect to each other.

> But with growing visibility, we're now seeing increased attention in the political sphere, targeting trans people and our rights to access basic things like housing, medical care, all kinds of things. So not purely a good trend. But definitely, there are good parts of it.

We are in a particularly critical moment for trans students, as trans and non-binary youth are under unprecedented legislative and policy attacks. In 2018, fewer than 20 anti-LGBTQ bills were introduced in state legislatures across the country. In 2022, more than 150 anti-LGBTQ bills were introduced. In 2023, more than 500 anti-LGBTQ bills were introduced.[4] Many of these bills would make it more difficult for trans people to change their names, make it difficult or impossible for trans youth to access gender-affirming medical care, ban trans athletes from participating in sports as their authentic selves, require teachers to jeopardize student safety by outing students, and more.

In some places, these anti-equality laws explicitly limit what educators can and can't say to students, such as Florida's "Don't Say Gay" bill, which specified: "Classroom instruction by school personnel or third parties on sexual orientation or gender identity may not occur in kindergarten through grade 3 or in a manner that is not age-appropriate or developmentally appropriate for students in accordance with state standards." Then, in April 2023, Florida expanded this bill to cover all grade levels, meaning discussion of sexual orientation and gender identity are banned for K–12 students in Florida. But studies have found that kids as young as three years old retain their expressed gender identity as they mature—which is a fancy way of saying, "Yes, they are really trans."[5]

Under Florida law, however, educators may be required to use the wrong name and pronouns for a trans student, lest the teacher be forced to provide "classroom instruction . . . on gender identity." Educators working with older students may still experience a chilling effect from the legislation, and those educators may not be certain what behaviors or topics of conversation are or aren't permitted under the law. While LGBTQ advocates are continuing to fight the bill in court, they have had mixed luck so far and, as of March 2023, the case is still awaiting an appeal.[6] In Chapter 7: Disrupt, we talk more about what educators can do to respond to anti-trans legislation.

Danica Roem (she/her), a transgender advocate and member of the Virginia House of Delegates, lamented the "demonization that we've seen of trans kids specifically, and LGBTQ kids more broadly . . . number one, you're talking about children, and they [opponents of trans equality] are singling out and stigmatizing the most vulnerable people that these elected officials represent in the first place. So they're attacking their constituents, and you cannot serve your constituents when you're attacking them. And number two, [opponents of trans equality are] trying to establish a precedent that the existence of trans kids is wrong."[7]

The Broader LGBTQ Community Needs Support

Hopefully, for most educators, the preceding clear needs identified are reason enough to support trans and non-binary students. But broader support—for all LGBQ students, whether or not they are trans—is also crucial.

Absence of support may stem from a simple lack of knowledge or it may be part of a larger campaign against LGBTQ rights. Either way, schools and policymakers have a responsibility to take action. When Sarah McBride (she/her), transgender advocate and State Senator for Delaware's First District, spoke with us, she stressed that "elected officials [in Delaware] have a constitutional and moral obligation to make sure that every student is able to access a safe and quality public education in our state. That is a universal responsibility and obligation, but it's heightened for students who are vulnerable and marginalized, including LGBTQ students. And so we are not doing our jobs, we are not fulfilling our oaths, unless we are building school communities that are welcoming and safe for LGBTQ students, as well as LGBTQ educators, staff, and LGBTQ family members of students. Regardless of what one personally thinks about LGBTQ identities, or LGBTQ rights, we are not doing our job if we don't guarantee those safe and affirming environments for LGBTQ students to be able to focus on what their job is at school, which is to learn and to grow and to thrive."

All Students Deserve to Be Their Authentic Selves

"One of the things that I'm really trying to help educators understand is that schools are harmful for cisgender folks and transgender folks. This isn't about [an adult's] perception that, 'Oh, we only have one of those students.' But all of the students are grappling with gender in some shape or form. We all need to be more savvy about how damaging it can be to have gender norms that limit who we can be."

—Dr. Melinda M. Mangin (she/her),
Transgender Students in Elementary School

Supporting LGBTQ students can also have a positive impact on an entire school community. McBride explained that trans-affirming policies also help students "with LGBTQ family members, students perceived to be LGBTQ, or any student who at any point deviates from rigid gender norms or breaks through these oppressive gender stereotypes, which is essentially every student."

The best available research backs up the view that affirming policies for LGBTQ students benefit not only those LGBTQ students but the whole school community. Dr. Kathleen Ethier (she/her), Director of the Division of Adolescent and School Health at the Centers for Disease Control (CDC), has looked into the policies and practices a school can put in place to support LGBTQ students, including "having GSAs, identifying safe spaces, having anti-harassment policies that are enumerated and enforced, and providing professional development for teachers," and found that "in the schools that put those policies and practices in place, [they] not only saw improvements in experience of violence, mental health and suicidality among LGBTQ kids, but also among students who identified as [not LGBTQ]."[8] Ethier continued:

> One of the most important things that schools can do is to provide a sense of what's called school connectedness, the belief that adults in your school care about you, care about your well-being, are interested in your success, want you to succeed. There's 20 years of research on school connectedness and when young people feel connected in their schools, 20 years later—into their late 20s and early 30s—we see an impact on everything from sexual health to use of substances to violence perpetration and experience of violence, mental health, and suicide.[9] So it is this really powerful, protective factor that speaks to the power of schools in shaping the trajectory of young people's lives.
>
> In some of our most recent research, we found that young people who identify as lesbian, gay or bisexual, or say that they're questioning their sexual orientation, and students who experience racism are the two groups of students who are least likely to say that they feel connected to others at school.[10] And so what that means for those groups of young people is not just the way that it impacts them on a daily basis, but it means that you don't have that protective factor that has the likelihood of that 20 year impact.
>
> So we are setting LGBTQ young people, and also students who experience racism at school, to have a different trajectory than their peers. And we owe it to those kids to not send them off to a different adulthood than their peers.

We spoke with Terrance TJ Johnson (he/him) who is based in Florida. Johnson is an Education and Inclusion Specialist at the YES! Institute, whose mission is to "prevent suicide and ensure the healthy development of all youth through powerful communication and education on gender and orientation." TJ is worried about the harm Florida's "Don't Say Gay" bill will cause. He also echoed a concern shared by other experts we spoke to, that a lack of support for trans youth in school "can lead to higher rates of mental illness, higher rates of suicide ideation, and just creating a space where people just don't feel like they can live being their authentic selves."

On the other hand, TJ stressed that "when you create a space where you do have that belonging created there, that inclusivity created there, you're lessening the amount of suicidal ideation, you're allowing students to develop a sense of self-worth."

Trans Joy

As a transgender person, what brings me joy is seeing other trans youth and trans adults flourish, and being happy in their day-to-day life.

—Daniel (he/him), 14[11]

Becoming an Advocate Educator

Acting as an Advocate Educator requires identifying the needs of trans students—whether or not there are already out trans students in a particular school—and practically and pragmatically working to ensure those needs are met. Advocacy may require rocking the boat or pushing back against the way things have always been done.

It can also be tempting to wait for the perfect moment to take action, when you've done all the research there is to do, all your allies are ready, and you've prepared an answer for every possible question. Unfortunately, as the old saying goes, "perfect is the enemy of good." If you wait until everything is exactly right, you may never get started at all!

We recommend that you take a moment to reflect on what these ideas mean to you:

- Why did you become an educator?

- What do you believe about children and learning?

- How have issues of gender and gender diversity shown up in your professional work?

- What is your comfort level in discussing these issues with students? Colleagues? Parents and community members?

- What do you think it would mean for YOU to be an advocate educator?

This book uses four core principles—Educate, Affirm, Include, and Disrupt—to categorize the types of actions schools can take to support trans and non-binary students. But these concepts overlap, meaning ideas from one chapter often connect to ideas from other chapters. In an ideal world, all four of the core principles would be implemented simultaneously, with strong education happening alongside the implementation of affirming policies and practices happening alongside inclusive classrooms; and curricula happening alongside the disruption of potential difficulties at the classroom, school, and community levels. Likewise, any strict division between the core principles is somewhat arbitrary: creating an inclusive classroom will require disrupting and redirecting disruptive students, disrupting potential difficulties will require educating staff, and so on.

Realistically, though, there are only so many hours in a day, and it's easy to get overwhelmed by how much you could do and use that as an excuse for not doing anything at all. (We can certainly think of times when we've looked at a long list of chores, decided they were all too much, and took a nap instead.) Give yourself permission to determine what will work best for you and your school community, rather than dividing things into strict categories.

Similarly, while this book is focused on supporting trans students, we shouldn't forget that trans adults in school communities may need our support as well.

Dr. Harper Keenan (he/him) is an assistant professor in the Department of Curriculum and Pedagogy at the University of British Columbia Faculty of Education. He founded the Trans Educators Network (TEN), which has done some of the only focused research into the experiences of trans educators. "For those of us who are concerned with supporting trans students," Keenan said, "we need to be aware that trans educators are not currently very well supported. And if trans adults are not able to thrive in schools, then trans kids are less able to thrive."

Tweak as Needed

This book contains tools for your toolbox, but no one tool will be right for every situation. While we can offer thoughts and suggestions about the needs of trans and non-binary students *in general*, we can't tell you the specific needs and priorities of the specific trans or non-binary students in your community, school, or classroom. Continue working with trans and non-binary youth, and don't assume that what students have needed in the past will be the same as what they need today.

One example of schools responding to the shifting needs of students is the structure and function of school GSAs. Historically standing for Gay-Straight Alliance, but increasingly standing for things like Genders and Sexualities Alliances, GSAs are extracurricular groups that provide space for LGBTQ students and allies to socialize, plan events, and build community. They're also places that are slowly being remade to better serve historically marginalized communities of trans youth and of LGBTQ youth of color. As one study noted, "Gen Z GSA students have begun to reimagine their clubs as if they were built from the ground up, with the needs of transgender students and students of color placed at their center. GSAs remain a critical but underdeveloped resource for learning how to recognize and challenge intersectional forms of interpersonal and institutional marginalization."[12]

Similarly, no student is "too young" to learn how to respect their peers, even if the exact language or lesson plan being used by educators will be different with a group of first-grade students than with a group of high schoolers. Transgender activist Gavin Grimm (he/him) had these words of wisdom for trans and non-binary youth of any age:

> You don't have to sit and bow to adults who are hurting you, or making the wrong decisions regarding your safety and health and happiness. Just because they're adults; you might be a kid, you don't know everything, that's fine. But you understand your emotions, you understand what you're feeling and what you're needing. And if the adults in your life—whether it's a school board, or even family—are not providing you with your needs, every child should feel like they have the right to voice those feelings, without being dismissed for being children.

You Got This!

> "They [trans and non-binary kids] are some of the bravest people I've ever met. My biggest takeaway is that these kids are so brave, and I need to be braver and bolder to support them."
> —Cheryl Greene (she/her), Director of HRC's Welcoming Schools

Educators and school leaders are already experts at supporting their students and creating healthy learning environments. While the specific needs of trans and non-binary students may be different than their cisgender peers, the end goal is the same: creating a safe and affirming learning environment where every student can thrive.

Celebrating trans and non-binary students also does not mean we have to erase gender entirely. Instead, we need more freedom to paint outside the lines. As author and expert Melinda Mangin put it, "When you're a teacher, you're teaching learners and you're thinking about, where are they coming from? What knowledge are they coming in with? Where do I want to bring them? And really, gender isn't relevant to any of it. They're learners, right? They bring identities that are important, and we want to know the whole child, but the way that we categorize children—and make gender a defining aspect of who we see—is really problematic. But we don't want to end gender, we want to have gender-full lives where gender is expansive, where you can celebrate lots of different gender expressions simultaneously, and they're not contradictory."

Educators and communities across the country are already building this gender-full world of support and acceptance. Dr. Kristina Olson (she/her), with Princeton University's TransYouth Project, found that when families are "able to get [their trans child] to a school that's at least mostly supportive, and in a community that's mostly supportive," most of those children thrive. In fact, she found "hundreds of [trans] youth who are doing really well in these supportive environments," indicating that it isn't simply being trans that puts youth at risk, it's being trans *and not receiving affirmation and support* that puts youth at risk.

A world where all trans youth are supported? That's what we're working toward—and we know others feel the same.

Putting It into Practice

Keep in mind that this work may bring up uncomfortable topics or conversations, and that's okay. In this space at the end of every chapter are ways to cement the information in this book: both personal reflection questions to ask yourself and scenarios to consider about addressing real-world challenges. We encourage you to take some time to reflect and catch your breath before taking action.

Personal Reflection Questions

1. Why did you choose to read this book?
2. What's your current knowledge and comfort level around trans and non-binary identity and topics?

Addressing Real-World Challenges

1. Knowing that collecting accurate information from groups of students can be difficult, how might you plan to survey or collect data about trans and non-binary students in your community?
2. Knowing what is important to students in your setting is critical to ensuring you can make a plan to support them. How might you go about finding out what issues and needs trans and non-binary students have in your school/district/state?
3. With your current level of knowledge, what resources or information do you need to better support trans and non-binary students?
4. Given your current role and situation, what real-world challenges does this section bring up for you in your community? How might you approach those challenges? What resources currently exist from your school/district/board of education to handle these challenges?
5. If your current role changed, how might your thoughts on these challenges change? Think about how you might answer differently as a classroom teacher, a school principal, a district administrator, and so on.

Notes

1. *National Survey on LGBTQ Youth Mental Health 2021*, The Trevor Project, n.d., https://www.thetrevorproject.org/wp-content/uploads/2021/05/The-Trevor-Project-National-Survey-Results-2021.pdf.

2. *National Survey on LGBTQ Youth Mental Health 2021.*

3. Kim Parker, Juliana Menasce Horowitz, and Anna Brown, "Americans' complex views on gender identity and transgender issues," Pew Research Center, June 28, 2022, https://www.pewre search.org/social-trends/2022/06/28/americans-complex-views-on-gender-identity-and-transgender-issues/.

4. Culllen Peele, "Roundup of Anti-LGBTQ+ Legislation Advancing In States Across the Country," Human Rights Campaign, May 23, 2023, https://www.hrc.org/press-releases/roundup-of-anti-lgbtq-legislation-advancing-in-states-across-the-country.

5. Jaclyn Diaz, "Florida's governor signs controversial law opponents dubbed 'Don't Say Gay,'" *NPR*, last updated March 28, 2022, https://www.npr.org/2022/03/28/1089221657/dont-say-gay-florida-desantis; Anthony Izaguirre and Brendan Farrington, "Florida expands 'Don't Say Gay'; House OKs anti-LGBTQ bills," *AP News*, April 19, 2023, https://apnews.com/article/desantis-florida-dont-say-gay-ban-684ed25a303f83208a89c5 56543183cb; Lindsey Tanner (Associated Press), "Transgender kids tend to maintain their identities as they grow up, study suggests," *PBS NewsHour*, May 4, 2022, https://www.pbs.org/newshour/nation/transgender-kids-tend-to-maintain-their-identities-as-they-grow-up-study-suggests.

6. Jim Saunders, " An appeals court will hear a challenge to Florida's law restricting instruction on gender identity," WUSF Public Media, March 28, 2023, https://wusfnews.wusf.usf.edu/courts-law/2023-03-28/appeals-court-challenge-florida-law-restricting-instruction-gender-identity.

7. Roem is also the former vocalist for heavy metal band Cab Ride Home and continues to be a "metalhead." When asked by the authors for advice on getting into heavy metal, Roem replied, "Well, everyone should always start with Black Sabbath, specifically their first two albums. For people in the modern day, one of the bands I've referenced a lot in my book [*Burn the Page: A True Story of Torching Doubts, Blazing Trails, and Igniting Change*] is Lacuna Coil. They're

a gothic metal band out of Milan, Italy. And the band I always fall back on, of course, is Metallica."

8. "Gay-Straight/Genders & Sexualities Alliances," Centers for Disease Control and Prevention, last reviewed October 26, 2021, https://www.cdc.gov/healthyyouth/safe-supportive-environments/sexuality-alliances.htm.

9. "School Connectedness," American Psychological Association, 2014, https://www.apa.org/pi/lgbt/programs/safe-supportive/school-connectedness.

10. Sanjana Pampati, Jack Andrzejewski, Ganna Sheremenko, Michelle Johns, Catherine A. Lesesne, and Catherine N. Rasberry, "School climate among transgender high school students: An exploration of school connectedness, perceived safety, bullying, and absenteeism," *Journal of School Nursing 36*, no. 4 (2020): 293–303, https://doi.org/10.1177/1059840518818259; "Adolescent Behaviors and Experiences Survey (ABES)," Centers for Disease Control and Prevention, last reviewed March 31, 2022, https://www.cdc.gov/healthyyouth/data/abes.htm.

11. Daniel (he/him), 14, quoted in "Trans day of visibility: 7 trans people share what brings them joy" by Fortesa Latifi, *Teen Vogue*, March 31, 2022, https://www.teenvogue.com/story/transgender-day-of-visibility-joy.

12. Madelaine Adelman, Sean Nonnenmacher, Bailey Borman, and Joseph G. Kosciw, "Gen Z GSAs: Trans-affirming and racially inclusive gender-sexuality alliances in secondary schools," *Teachers College Record: The Voice of Scholarship in Education* 124, no. 8 (September 2022): 192–219, https://doi.org/10.1177/016146812211231.

Setting the Stage

CHAPTER ONE

Background Information

"The kid that's most marginalized in the classroom, if my classroom or my school can be a safe space for them, then everybody else is gonna be fine. If we make the school safe and affirming and a great space to learn for the most marginalized, everybody else will be okay, too. So that's what I aspire to do."

—Tim'm West (he/they), Executive Director at the LGBTQ Institute at the National Center for Civil and Human Rights

WHEN DID you first hear the word *transgender*? Who was the first out transgender person you met? When did you first encounter a student or other young person who was trans?

Many of us, particularly those who were born before the era of Google and Facebook, first learned about trans people on daytime talk shows—if we learned about trans people at all. We almost certainly didn't have teachers who spoke about trans people in grade school. Trans people might have merited attention in higher education, but almost certainly as a minor mention in a single chapter or two, and not as a nuanced and complex community. Likewise, many of us were well into adulthood before we met our first out trans person.

A Brief History of Trans Identity

According to one 2021 survey, less than half of the people living in the United States know someone who is transgender or who uses gender-neutral pronouns.[1] And while that's significantly more people than noted in previous surveys, it still means there are still huge parts of the population that simply don't know trans people. Meanwhile, a 2022 survey found that two-thirds of Americans "say they've had a paranormal encounter," which may mean that more people in the United States think they've met a ghost than know a trans person, demonstrating a wide gap in basic awareness of trans identity.[2] (These surveys also leave important questions unanswered, including, "But what if the ghost was trans?")

These facts—a lack of education about trans identity and a lack of interaction with *out* trans people—can lead many to assume that transgender identity is new, that the experiences of trans people are taking society into uncharted territory, and that there is little history or experience to guide us as we consider how to best support transgender students. Fortunately, this is not the case.

It is true that words like *transgender* and *genderqueer*—as well as terms like *gender binary* and *LGBTQ* (or the even longer *LGBTQIA+*)—came into existence in the 19th and 20th centuries, with many of these terms less than 100 years old.[3] That makes it difficult (if not impossible) to apply modern terms to people who lived hundreds or thousands of years ago. It also may not make sense to use English terms like *transgender* to refer to people who today live in other societies and cultures. At the same time, there have always been people who exist outside of the static boxes "male" and "female." At every point in history, and in every society that exists today, we can find people living gender-expansive lives as vibrant and thriving members of their community (see Figure 1.1).

This section is not intended to be a complete history of gender, or of trans identity. Julian Gill-Peterson's *Histories of the Transgender Child* has extensive information on the formation of modern ideas about trans youth. Also, Appendix 1: Additional

FIGURE 1.1   Ginny Suss, photograph from Trans Prom featuring youth activist Danielle Trujillo holding a sign that reads "trans kids have always existed," 2023.[4]

Resources includes lots of materials for learning about trans identity and trans history more broadly. Rather, this section is intended as an antidote to the false claim that being trans is new or was somehow created by the Western world. In fact, trans people have always been a part of humanity, even if the words used to talk about gender identity have changed (and are changing, and will continue changing) over time.

One of the earliest examples of a trans-*ish* identity or experience (i.e., identities and experiences that seem related to the modern experience of being trans, even if the term *trans* isn't being used) comes from millennia ago: the Galli of ancient Rome, eunuch priests of the mother-goddess Cybele. Modern historians describe the Galli as "wearing bright clothes, heavy jewelry, make-up and sporting bleached and crimped hair," while the Roman writer Julius Firmicus Maternus, living in the 4th century CE, said, "[Galli] say they are not men, and indeed they aren't; they want to pass as women."[5]

In India and South Asia, the hijra community stretches back at least 1,000 years, although hijra have not always been accepted or supported, particularly by Western outsiders. Franciscan travelers in the 1650s harshly described "men and boys who dress like women" as a sign of depravity, and British colonizers attempted to extinguish hijra identity in the 1800s.[6] Nevertheless, strong hijra communities continue to exist throughout the region; Pakistan officially recognized hijra as a third sex in 2009; Bangladesh, in 2013; and India; in 2014. Today, it is estimated that more than 10 million hijra people live in the region.[7]

Meanwhile, in North America, many Indigenous communities use the umbrella term *two-spirit* to describe third-gender or otherwise gender-variant roles and identities that exist in many native cultures. The term *two-spirit* is often attributed to Elder Myra Laramee, who proposed its use in 1990 during the Third Annual Intertribal Native American, First Nations, Gay and Lesbian American Conference. There is not one single definition of *two-spirit*, and Indigenous populations may also have terms in their own languages for their two-spirit members. *Two-spirit* replaced the term *berdache*, which had been negatively used by colonizers and white anthropologists to describe Indigenous people since at least the 1600s.[8]

There has been a growth of two-spirit community gatherings and activism in recent decades, with Bay Area American Indian Two-Spirits (BAAITS) holding a large annual powwow since 2011 and aiming to "restore and recover the role of Two-Spirit people within the American Indian/First Nations community by creating a forum for the spiritual, cultural and artistic expression of Two-Spirit people." Likewise, two-spirit activists were heavily involved in resistance to the Dakota Access Pipeline and elsewhere; as two-spirit activist Jen Deerinwater wrote in 2018, "Reviving our stories, traditions, and roles as multi-gendered Indigenous people is how we resist our oppressors. It's how we will overcome settler colonialism and complete the sacred circle."[9]

Finally, there is a long history of women dressing as men to work in all-male professions, fight in all-male armies, or perhaps simply to live as their authentic selves. Charley Parkhurst, once described as "best whip in California," was born as Charlotte Parkhurst in 1812, but lived and worked as a man for decades, not being discovered until Parkhurst's death in 1879. Similarly,

Albert D. J. Cashier was born as Jennie Irene Hodgers in 1843, but adopted a male persona to enlist in the Union Army in 1862 and lived the rest of his life—more than 50 years—as a man.[10] Were these two people trans? Unfortunately we can't go back and ask them, but that they both continued to live as men for much of their lives suggests a more nuanced and complex answer than that they were simply women who wanted to work in male professions. (As a side note, it is recommended to not use a trans person's given name—sometimes referred to as a "deadname"—when referring to them. Because we don't know how Parkhurst or Cashier identified, we used both their given and chosen names.)

Looking specifically at language, the pioneering German sex and gender researcher Magnus Hirschfeld didn't create the term *transsexualismus* until 1923. The term was later Anglicized to *transsexualism* and *transsexual* by David Oliver Cauldwell in 1949 and 1950, while the word *transgender* didn't appear until 1965, when Dr. John Oliven argued that being trans was about more than just sexuality and that the term *transsexual* was too limiting.[11] Since then, there has been a rise in terms like *trans*, *genderqueer*, *gender fluid*, *non-binary*, and the many other ways to describe the complicated experiences of living in a gendered body.

Trans Joy

"Being part of the transgender community makes me feel not alone because I know there are other people like me."

—Griffin (she/her), 12

Language has changed, is changing, and will continue to change. While this ever-changing landscape can make it difficult to apply modern ideas of gender and identity to historical figures, we must also avoid the trap of thinking that trans or LGBTQ people didn't exist in the past simply because the language we use today was not yet invented.

(Some of) The Many Ways to Be Trans

So what do these historical terms, identities, and experiences teach us about trans people in the United States today?

First and foremost, they remind us that there is no One Right Way to Be Trans. Indeed, there are as many ways to be trans as there are members of the trans community. Some transgender people know from a very young age, as early as three or four, that their gender is somehow different from what the world seems to expect of them. Some people realize they're trans in adolescence, or around puberty. And some people don't discover their trans identity until well into adulthood.

Likewise, some trans people undergo medical procedures—hormones or surgery—to alter their body. Other trans people don't. Some trans people only change their name with friends and family, others legally change their name in court, and some trans people don't change their name at all. It's impossible to tell if someone is trans just by looking at them or by how they act. After all, if there's no One Right Way to Be Trans, there's also no one right way to look or act trans, either.

Just like there is no One Right Way to Be Trans, there is also no Hierarchy of Transness. That is, no trans person is any more trans or less trans than someone else. Realizing you're trans at an early age isn't better or worse than realizing you're trans later in life, just different. Likewise, specific interests or types of expression don't mean someone is more or less trans, or more or less of a "real" man, woman, or anything else. Similar to any other community, the trans community has people who like sports and people who don't, people who like makeup and jewelry and people who don't, people who want to be out and loud and proud and people who prefer to be quiet and far from the center of attention.

The same is true, then, of the needs of trans students. While there are overarching themes and similarities among the needs of trans students, this book can only provide guidance on what trans students require in general to be supported in school and to thrive as their authentic selves. We can't tell you what your specific students want and need. With that in mind, we encourage you to work with your students to determine their priorities, ask families what help they need, and evaluate your education community to find the approaches that will work best for your unique community.

Trans Joy

"I'd say my favorite part of my trans identity is that it's mine! It's a part of me and I wear it openly and proudly."

—Kameron (he/him), 17[12]

How Many Trans Students Are There?

"When I first started my research career, I couldn't focus on trans youth. It wasn't even a possibility to only focus on trans youth. All of the scholarship at that time focused on LGBT youth; we didn't have nuances. As a young trans scholar coming into the field, I annoyed everybody by being like, 'Well, wait, no, this is different for trans kids [than for cis kids].'"

—Russ Toomey (he/they), Professor of Human Development and Family Science at the University of Arizona

Researching LGBTQ+ populations can be difficult for a number of reasons, including a lack of questions about sexual orientation and gender identity (SOGI) on many existing large-scale population surveys (e.g., regular surveys conducted by the U.S. Department of Commerce or Department of Labor) and a lack of SOGI data in many existing administrative systems (e.g., a school district's student record database).[13]

Surveying young people is also tricky: conducting research on minors generally requires parental consent, young people are more difficult than adults to reach via landline phones, reaching cellphones is often harder and more expensive than calling landlines, and online surveys of youth often require a parent or guardian to start the survey and then hand it off to the young person. Some youth may also simply lie when surveyed, either because they are not comfortable sharing personal information with adults or simply because youth sometimes lie when taking surveys.[14] (One of the authors of this book definitely remembers lying on surveys she was given as a high school student!)

This lack of data is slowly changing, however. Massachusetts, for example, conducts a biannual Youth Risk Behavior Survey. In 2021, the most recent year for which data is available, that survey found that 5% of Massachusetts youth identified as transgender or said they were questioning their gender identity.[15] Likewise, the Centers for Disease Control and Prevention (CDC) has been asking young people about sexual orientation in the Youth Risk Behavior Survey since 2015, but will be adding a question about gender identity beginning in 2023. CDC researcher Dr. Kathleen Ethier, whose work is discussed in the Introduction, is excited to "finally have national data on trans youth [via the Youth Risk Behavior Survey], which will be fabulous."

But even with the limited data we have, it's clear that the existence of transgender youth is not a new phenomenon. As is discussed in the Introduction, transgender people have always existed, even if the word *transgender* did not yet exist. Still, the number of young people identifying as trans is on the rise, as are the number of young people identifying as part of the broader LGBTQ community.[16] This has resulted in anti-trans voices claiming that children are being fooled or tricked or peer pressured into being trans. To show why this fear is unfounded, we need to take a brief detour to discuss left- and right-handedness. Author and researcher Julia Serano explained it like this:

> During the twentieth century, in many Western countries, there was a precipitous rise in left-handedness. For instance, in Australia, the prevalence of left-handed people increased from 2.0 percent to a whopping 13.2 percent! Apparently, a social contagion

swept through these nations, and children suddenly began feeling peer pressure to experiment with handedness and to adopt left-handed identities. Then, the left-handed deviants began pushing their "left-hander agenda" in order to recruit . . . oh, wait, sorry, that's not what happened at all.

In actuality, left-handedness (like being transgender) is a part of human variation—both are pancultural trans-historical phenomena. In the case of left-handedness, roughly 10 to 12 percent of children inexplicably express this tendency from as early as infancy. In the beginning of the twentieth century, there was intense stigma targeting left-handedness, which led parents and schools to force all children to be right-handed, often against their intrinsic preferences (this still happens in many places). But eventually, there was a realization that this stigma was unnecessary and unfair, and people started letting children decide for themselves which hands to use. In other words, there wasn't really a rise in left-handedness so much as there was a rise in left-handed acceptance.

Granted, it's not a perfect analogy. For starters, I highly doubt that 10 to 12 percent of the population is predisposed toward being transgender! Also, it appears that children who display early left-handed tendencies can often be trained to use (perhaps even favor) their right hands without experiencing overwhelming dysphoria. (In contrast, we know from the countless trans narratives that I alluded to earlier, the same is not true for many trans people who are forced to adopt an unwanted gender.) Despite these differences, this parallel does hold true in the following sense: you don't need to concoct half-assed theories to explain the mysterious appearance of transgender children. All you need to do is recognize that we have always existed. It's just that we were long rendered invisible via stigma, punishment, and ostracization.[17]

Dr. Kristina Olson, an academic researcher with Princeton's TransYouth Project, has uncovered some of the best available evidence that trans youth absolutely know who they are:

> It's funny, I always say our main findings from [the TransYouth Project] are things that, if you know trans youth, are basically "duh" findings. But I'll repeat them, because sometimes there are points in which it is useful to have a scientific citation to say something that folks already know.
>
> One [finding] is that a youth cohort who identify [as genders other than the ones they were assigned at birth] very, very early in development—almost all by the age of four—the majority of those kids are very consistent in their gender identity. Our latest data are five years out from social transition, and we see that more than 90% identify still as binary trans youth, about 3.5% as non-binary youth (which for some of them felt like a change, or some of them didn't feel like a change [but] is a better label).
>
> Only about 2.5% are identifying as cisgender today, which we tend to refer as having "*re*-transitioned," without the loaded onus of the word *de*-transition. And we're still following them; our goal is to follow them for 20 years.
>
> So one [finding] is the general consistency of identity, with the recognition that that's obviously not going to be true for everyone.

Ultimately, researchers estimate that, out of every 100 young people in the United States, at least one or two are transgender. Specifically, a Williams Institute study found that 1.43% of 13- to 17-year-olds identify as trans, while a study from the CDC found an average of 1.8% of high school students identify as trans.[18] This means that there are hundreds of thousands of trans youth across the United States, in every city and state—if your school has 500 students, it's likely that at least a handful of them are trans (see Figure 1.2).

How Many Adults and Youth Identify as Transgender in the United States?| **10**

STATE	13-17 PERCENT	13-17 NUMBER	18-24 PERCENT	18-24 NUMBER	25-64 PERCENT	25-64 NUMBER	65+ PERCENT	65+ NUMBER	ALL ADULTS 18+ PERCENT	ALL ADULTS 18+ NUMBER
North Carolina	1.27%	8,500	2.46%	24,000	0.73%	38,400	0.53%	8,900	0.87%	71,300
Oklahoma	1.00%	2,600	2.52%	9,300	0.44%	8,500	0.19%	1,100	0.63%	18,900
South Carolina	1.14%	3,700	0.87%	4,100	0.43%	11,300	0.38%	3,500	0.47%	19,000
Tennessee	0.74%	3,100	1.95%	11,700	0.44%	15,000	0.09%	1,000	0.52%	27,700
Texas	1.42%	29,800	0.71%	19,800	0.42%	61,500	0.31%	11,600	0.43%	92,900
Virginia	1.18%	6,200	1.11%	8,800	0.40%	18,000	0.34%	4,600	0.47%	31,400
West Virginia	0.68%	700	1.18%	1,800	0.36%	3,200	0.22%	800	0.40%	5,700
NORTHEAST	1.82%	61,700	1.58%	80,600	0.48%	141,600	0.32%	31,600	0.57%	253,800
Connecticut	1.64%	3,700	1.35%	4,600	0.45%	8,300	0.38%	2,400	0.54%	15,300
Maine	1.59%	1,200	1.44%	1,600	0.47%	3,300	0.34%	1,000	0.53%	5,900
Massachusetts	1.44%	5,900	2.30%	15,700	0.44%	16,100	0.46%	5,400	0.67%	37,100
New Hampshire	0.84%	700	1.53%	1,900	0.48%	3,500	0.34%	900	0.57%	6,300
New Jersey	0.67%	3,800	1.67%	12,700	0.52%	24,800	0.38%	5,600	0.62%	43,100
New York	3.00%	34,800	1.37%	24,100	0.46%	47,600	0.31%	10,100	0.53%	81,800
Pennsylvania	1.30%	10,000	1.50%	16,900	0.51%	33,400	0.24%	5,600	0.55%	56,000
Rhode Island	1.93%	1,200	2.11%	2,300	0.54%	3,000	0.21%	400	0.66%	5,700
Vermont	1.33%	500	1.26%	800	0.48%	1,500	0.29%	400	0.53%	2,700

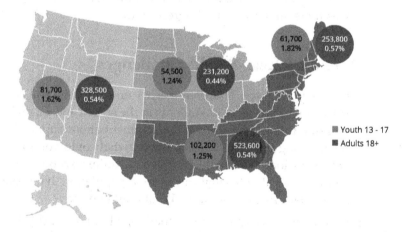

FIGURE 1.2 U.S. youth who identify as transgender.
Source: The Williams Institute, UCLA School of Law. For the complete chart of state population breakdowns, visit https://williamsinstitute.law.ucla.edu/subpopulations/transgender-people/

Putting It into Practice

Following are scenarios to consider about addressing real-world challenges and personal reflection questions to ask yourself. We encourage you to take some time to reflect and catch your breath before taking action.

Personal Reflection Questions

1. What training or education, if any, did you receive about how to support trans students?

2. What new information did you learn from this chapter? What did you already know?

3. Was any of the background information surprising to you? Was there anything you disagreed with?

Addressing Real-World Challenges

1. Let's say you're a classroom teacher and the principal says there are no transgender students in the school and therefore you don't need professional development about supporting them. Using this chapter as evidence, what could you say to your principal? Alternatively, let's say you're a school leader and the district notes that this is not a population that needs additional focus in your area. What might you say?

2. Given your current role and situation, what real-world challenges does this chapter bring up for you in your community? How might you approach those challenges? What resources currently exist from your school/district/board of education to handle these challenges?

3. If your current role changed, how would your thoughts on these challenges change? Think about how you might answer differently as a classroom teacher, a school principal, a district administrator, and so on.

Notes

1. Rachel Minkin and Anna Brown, "Rising shares of U.S. adults know someone who is transgender or goes by gender-neutral pronouns," Pew Research Center, July 27, 2021, https://www .pewresearch.org/short-reads/2021/07/27/rising-shares-of-u-s-adults-know-someone-who-is-transgender-or-goes-by-gender-neutral-pronouns/.

2. Taylor Orth, "Two-thirds of Americans say they've had a paranormal encounter," YouGov, October 20, 2022, https://today .yougov.com/topics/society/articles-reports/2022/10/20/ americans-describe-paranormal-encounters-poll.

3. Erin Blakemore, "From LGBT to LGBTQIA+: The evolving recognition of identity," *National Geographic*, October 19, 2021, https:// www.nationalgeographic.com/history/article/from-lgbt-to-lgbtqia-the-evolving-recognition-of-identity.

4. Ginny Suss, photograph from Trans Prom featuring youth activist Danielle Trujillo holding a sign that reads "trans kids have always existed," 2023.

5. Shelley Hales, "Looking for eunuchs: The Galli and Attis in Roman art," in *Eunuchs in antiquity and beyond*, ed. Shaun Tougher (Swansea: Classical Press of Wales and Duckworth, 2002), p. 91; Julius Firmicus Maternus, *De errore profanarum religionum (The Error of the Pagan Religions)*, trans. Clarence A. Forbes (New York: Newman Press, 1970), p. 51, https://archive.org/details/firmicus-maternus.

6. Nalini Iyer, "Hijra," *Encyclopedia of Gender and Society*, Volume 1 (SAGE, 2009), p. 421; Donald Lach, *Asia in the Making of Europe*, Volume III: A Century of Advance. Book 2 (South Asia. University of Chicago Press, 1998); Jessica Hinchy, *Governing Gender and Sexuality in Colonial India: The Hijra*, c. 1850–1900, (Cambridge University Press, 2019).

7. Basim Usmani, "Pakistan to register 'third sex' hijras," *The Guardian*, 18 July 2009; Mohosinul Karim, "Hijras now a separate gender,"

Dhaka Tribune, November 11, 2013; "India recognises transgender people as third gender," *The Guardian*. April 15, 2014; Jeff Roy, "Unveiling Koovagam," *World Policy Journal*, 2009, 31 (2): 93.

8. "Two-Spirit Community," Re:searching for LGBTQ Health, University of Toronto Dalla Lana School of Public Health and Centre for Addiction and Mental Health, n.d., https://lgbtqhealth.ca/community/two-spirit.php; "Two-Spirit," Indian Health Service, U.S. Department of Health and Human Services, n.d., https://www.ihs.gov/lgbt/health/twospirit/; Kylan Mattias de Vries, "Berdache (Two-Spirit)," in *Encyclopedia of Gender and Society*, ed. Jodi O'Brien (Los Angeles: SAGE Publications, 2009), p. 64.

9. "Bay Area American Indian Two-Spirits (BAAITS)," n.d., https://www.baaits.org/about; Jen Deerinwater, "Our pride: Honoring and recognizing our two spirit past and present," Rewire News Group, June 5, 2018, https://rewirenewsgroup.com/2018/06/05/pride-honoring-recognizing-two-spirit-past-present/.

10. Heather Thomas, "Women who dressed as men and made history," Library of Congress Blogs: Headlines and Heroes: Newspapers, Comics and More Fine Print, March 30, 2021, https://blogs.loc.gov/headlinesandheroes/2021/03/women-who-dressed-as-men-and-made-history/; Kirstin Cronn-Mills, *Transgender Lives: Complex Stories, Complex Voices* (Minneapolis: Lerner Publishing Group, 2014), p. 41.

11. David Oliver Cauldwell, *Questions and Answers on the Sex Life and Sexual Problems of Trans-Sexuals . . .* (Girard, KS: Haldeman-Julius Publications, 1950); John F. Oliven, *Sexual Hygiene and Pathology* (Philadelphia: Lippincott, 1965), p. 514, cited in Cristan Williams, "Transgender," *Transgender Studies Quarterly* (TSQ), nos. 1–2 (May 2014): 232–234, https://doi.org/10.1215/23289252-2400136.

12. Kameron (he/him), 17, quoted in "Trans day of visibility: 7 trans people share what brings them joy" by Fortesa Latifi, *Teen Vogue*, March 31, 2022, https://www.teenvogue.com/story/transgender-day-of-visibility-joy.

13. Kellan Baker, Laura E. Durso, and Aaron Ridings, "How to collect data about LGBT communities," Center for American Progress, March 15, 2016, https://www.americanprogress.org/article/how-to-collect-data-about-lgbt-communities/

14. Amanda Lenhart, "The challenges of conducting surveys of youth," Pew Research Center, June 21, 2013, https://www.pewresearch.org/short-reads/2013/06/21/the-challenges-of-conducting-surveys-on-youths/; Anya Kamenetz, "'Mischievous responders' confound research on teens," NPR Ed, May 22, 2014, https://www.npr.org/sections/ed/2014/05/22/313166161/mischievous-responders-confound-research-on-teens.

15. Massachusetts Commission on Lesbian, Gay, Bisexual, Transgender, Queer, and Questioning Youth. (2023). Massachusetts Commission on LGBTQ Youth: Report and Recommendations for Fiscal Year 2024. Retrieved from https://www.mass.gov/annual-recommendations.

16. Eesha Pendharkar, "Number of trans youth is twice as high as previous estimates, study finds," *Education Week*, June 14, 2022, https://www.edweek.org/leadership/number-of-trans-youth-is-twice-as-high-as-previous-estimates-study-finds/2022/06; Jeffrey M. Jones, "U.S. LGBT identification steady at 7.2%," Gallup, February 22, 2023, https://news.gallup.com/poll/470708/lgbt-identification-steady.aspx.

17. Julia Serano, "Transgender agendas, social contagion, peer pressure, and prevalence," *Medium*, November 27, 2017, https://juliaserano.medium.com/transgender-agendas-social-contagion-peer-pressure-and-prevalence-c3694d11ed24.

18. Jody L. Herman, Andrew R. Flores, and Kathryn K. O'Neill, *How Many Adults and Youth Identify as Transgender in the United States?* The Williams Institute, UCLA School of Law, June 2022, https://williamsinstitute.law.ucla.edu/publications/trans-adults-united-states/; Michelle M. Johns, Richard Lowry, Jack Andrzejewski, Lisa C. Barrios, Zewditu Demissie, Timothy McManus, Catherine N.

Rasberry, Leah Robin, and J. Michael Underwood, "Transgender identity and experiences of violence victimization, substance use, suicide risk, and sexual risk behaviors among high school students: 19 states and large urban school districts, 2017," *Morbidity and Mortality Weekly Report (MMWR)* 68, no. 3 (January 25, 2019): 67–71, CDC, 31://dx.doi.org/10.15585/mmwr.mm6803a3.

CHAPTER TWO

Glossary of Terms and Definitions

"Folks are very fixated on language. And so I do a lot of work in professional development to try to simplify language, and also to invite folks in to be a longtime learner around language and to just shift our understanding. We are not the experts on [other people's experiences], and that is okay."

—Bex Mui (she/her),
Director of Stonewall National Education Project

IT CAN be tempting to view a list of terms and definitions as a homework assignment: memorize the terms, take the test, and— once the memorization is complete—you've achieved a true understanding of the topic. Real people are more complicated and nuanced than dictionary definitions, though, so don't take anything in this chapter (or, indeed, in this book) to be inflexible, completely universal, or written in stone. There will inevitably be people who use terms in different ways, and language changes over time. If someone in your life uses language in a way that's unfamiliar to you, or in a way that contradicts your understanding of a word or phrase, we encourage you to ask, "What does that term mean to you?" You might also offer, "Here's my understanding of that word. Is that how you're using it?"

Nevertheless, definitions can provide some common ground, so we're including a list of definitions to some of the most relevant language used throughout this book. But remember: language should be a flexible tool to help us understand each other and find common ground, not an inflexible barrier used to exclude or create divisions.

Many of the definitions in this chapter require use of other terms that are defined here; these will be formatted in SMALL CAPS.

GENDER IDENTITY: A person's internal sense of their own gender, whether or not it matches their sex assigned at birth. Everyone (including you, dear reader!) has a gender identity. For those whose sex assigned at birth aligns with their gender identity (i.e., people who are not transgender; see CISGENDER entry), they may never have considered when and how and why they came to understand their gender as they do. If you've never thought about your gender or gender identity before, we encourage you to do so! Some questions to consider:[1]

- Thinking about yourself today, how do you know you're a man, a woman, or something else entirely?

- As a child, when did you first realize others saw you as a boy or a girl? Did it match how you thought about yourself?

- Is there anything you do (behaviors, ways of dressing, how you talk, etc.) only because people expect "real" men or women to act a certain way?

TRANS/TRANSGENDER: Anyone whose GENDER IDENTITY doesn't match their SEX ASSIGNED AT BIRTH. In this book, *trans* and *transgender* are used as umbrella terms that include non-binary people—even though not every non-binary person self-identifies as trans—because the issues facing trans and non-binary communities (and the ways educators and allies can support these communities) are substantially similar. The longer term *transgender* is generally interchangeable with *trans*.

Some trans people transition, while others do not; whether or not someone is trans does not depend on whether or not they want to or are able to transition. (See TRANSITION.)

GENDER BINARY: The idea that all human beings fall into one of two mutually exclusive and narrowly defined categories: female and male.

NON-BINARY: Someone who identifies as neither male nor female, or identifies as both male and female, or whose gender identity doesn't align with the idea of a binary gender in the first place. The issues facing the non-binary community and trans community are very similar when it comes to general respect and understanding: access to safe and affirming education, legal rights and restrictions, access to medical treatment, and overall experiences of support and discrimination. As such, for the purposes of this book, we use *trans* to be inclusive of non-binary people, even though not every individual trans or non-binary person will agree with that definition.

Non-binary is sometimes written as nonbinary or non binary, or shortened to enby. (Some people also use NB as shorthand for non-binary, but NB can also mean "non-Black," as in NBPOC to mean "non-Black people of color," so we recommend using enby instead.[2]) In addition, some people dislike the term *non-binary* because it defines someone by what they're *not* rather than what they *are*. People who feel that way may prefer terms like gender-queer, gender fluid, or agender. Language and identity can be nuanced and complicated, so the most important thing to remember is that you should refer to people using whatever terms they prefer.

Trans Joy

The best thing about being non-binary is being able to combine aspects of different genders and make your own gender that's just *you.*

—Ian (they/them), 11

SEX ASSIGNED AT BIRTH: When we're born, a doctor says, "It's a girl!" or "It's a boy!" This almost always happens without any sort of genetic testing or chromosomal analysis, and certainly doesn't involve asking the baby what they think of being called a boy or a girl. For most people, their sex assigned at birth matches their gender identity, meaning they are what is termed CISGENDER. If someone's sex assigned at birth does not match their GENDER IDENTITY, they are TRANS.

In the introduction, we referenced a 2022 survey that found more and more people in the United States favor protecting transgender people from the abstract idea of "discrimination," but also that more and more people believe gender is solely determined by someone's sex at birth. This is a contradiction because a trans person's gender identity and gender expression may not match their sex assigned at birth, meaning it's not possible to protect trans people from discrimination while simultaneously classifying all people based on what a doctor said when the person was born.

GENDER EXPRESSION: How someone shares (or does not share) their gender with the world via clothing, makeup, hair, and more. We can't fully know or understand someone's gender identity simply by looking at their outward appearance. Gender expression varies among different cultures around the world, and we all make small and large changes to our outward appearance throughout the course of our lives.

TRANSSEXUAL: An older term that is often used as a synonym for transgender. Some people use transsexual to specifically mean a trans person who desires to medically transition; using this definition, all transsexual people are transgender, but not all trans people are transsexual.

ALLIES: Supporters. Accomplices. Partners in crime. Being an ally is an active process, not a static identity. Being an ally doesn't mean you're perfect, or that you never mess up, but it does mean you keep on trying even when it's difficult.

CISGENDER: Someone whose gender identity aligns with their sex assigned at birth. Most people in the world are probably cisgender. While it's not super important for individuals to consider whether or not they are cisgender, it's incredibly important to be able to talk about the differences in overall experience when trans people access education, interact with law enforcement, etc. There is a generally unspoken assumption in the United States that everyone is cis; for example, cis students are more likely to see themselves represented in classroom curriculum than trans students, doctors are more likely to understand cis bodies than trans bodies, cis people are more likely to have legal documents that reflect their gender than trans people, and so on. Cisgender is sometimes shortened to cis.

GENDER DYSPHORIA: The distress that trans people may feel when their gender identity doesn't align with their sex assigned at birth, with how other people perceive them, and/ or how they perceive themselves. The *Diagnostic and Statistical Manual of Mental Disorders, Fifth Edition (DSM V)* defines gender dysphoria as a "marked incongruence between their experienced or expressed gender and the one they were assigned at birth."[3]

GENDER EXPANSIVE, GENDER VARIANT, and GENDER NONCONFORMING (GNC): Terms used to talk about the broader community of people who may not identify as trans, but also feel restricted by gendered roles and expectations. These terms are sometimes used in phrases like "trans and gender expansive people" as a way to talk about anyone who doesn't fit neatly into gendered roles and expectations.

QUEER: An umbrella term for anyone who is not cisgender and heterosexual, sometimes used as an alternative to acronyms like LGBT or LGBTQ or LGBTQIA+. Individuals may also identify their sexuality as "queer," similar to gay, straight, and so on. Queer has historically been used as a slur, and its use today is not universal—some people find the reclaimed use of queer to be empowering, while others strongly disagree.[4]

INTERSEX/DISORDERS OF SEXUAL DEVELOPMENT (DSD): When a person's physical body—their chromosomes or their hormones or how their genitals developed—doesn't align with societal expectations for how either a male or female body "should" work. What has in the past been called hermaphrodite, a medically inaccurate term that was often used in mean or hurtful ways. Not all intersex people, or people with DSD, identify as part of the broader LGBTQ community, but many of the forms of discrimination the communities face are similar.

LESBIAN: A woman who primarily experiences attraction to other women.

GAY: Someone who primarily experiences attraction to other people of the same gender. Sometimes used specifically to describe men who primarily experience attraction to other men.

SAME GENDER LOVING (SGL): A term created by African American activist Cleo Manago in the 1990s as an Afrocentric alternative to what were seen as white- or Euro-centric terms like *gay* or *lesbian*.

BISEXUAL/BI: Someone whose sexual attraction is not limited to one gender. The term bisexual is generally *not* meant to exclude trans people or otherwise be used in transphobic ways, but some people prefer terms like *pansexual* or *omnisexual* (both meaning someone whose attraction is not limited by gender) as a way to explicitly frame their sexuality outside of a gender binary.

LGBT(QIA+): The ever-growing list of lesbian, gay, bisexual, trans, queer, intersex, asexual, and more. One of the reasons *queer* has become more popular is because it's shorter and simpler than listing a bunch of letters.

ASEXUAL: Someone who experiences little or no sexual attraction; sometimes shortened to ace.

AROMANTIC: Someone who experiences little or no romantic attraction; sometimes shortened to aro.

PRONOUNS: Words used to refer to someone when not using a name, for example, *he*, *she*, or *they*. Many (but not all!) trans people use pronouns that are different from those that align with their sex assigned at birth. Using someone's correct name and pronouns is important regardless of whether or not they are trans, but is particularly important when working with trans students. It may take practice to use new or different pronouns than you did in the past, but it is an important part of being an ally. The most common English pronouns in use today are:

- **He/him/his** for boys and men, for example, "Slate walked to the store to buy something, but he forgot his wallet."

- **She/her/hers** for girls and women, for example, "Dedra planned to bike to the store, but her bike had a flat so she couldn't go."

- **They/them/theirs** for both groups of people, for example, "Slate and Dedra decided they would rather see a movie instead of going to the store," *and* for individuals as a gender-neutral pronoun, for example, "Slate and Dedra's friend

Aidan asked to go to the movies, too. Aidan had recently moved to town and they were looking for new friends."

Using *they* for a single person may be new for some people, and may not match what you were taught in grammar school. Nevertheless, using *they* as a singular pronoun is validated by *The Chicago Manual of Style*, *Merriam-Webster Dictionary*, the *Oxford English Dictionary*, and the Associated Press, among others.[5]

Some people may use multiple pronouns, such as *he/they* or *they/she*. What this means in practice is unique to each person, but may mean that person likes switching pronouns depending on their feelings at the moment, or that they're experimenting with pronouns and not sure which ones feel right just yet. Asking someone what pronouns to use, and when (and then actually using those pronouns correctly!), can be a great way to demonstrate allyship.

NEOPRONOUNS: In addition to pronouns like *he*, *she*, and *they*, some people use gender-neutral or non-gendered pronouns that were created more recently, including *ze/zir/zirs*, *xe/xir/xirs*, and *fae/faer/faers*. While it is not important to memorize every possible neopronoun, it is important to respect the pronouns someone is using and call people what they ask to be called.[6]

TRANSITION (social, legal, medical): Broadly speaking, a trans person transitions when they shift from living as their SEX ASSIGNED AT BIRTH to living as their authentic self. There is no one way to transition, and every trans person's transition is somewhat different. Transitioning is often put into three categories: medical, and legal.

A **social transition** consists of shifting things that don't require medical intervention or legal changes, often including gender expression (clothing, hair, makeup, etc.) and using a new or different name and pronouns.

A **medical transition** consists of medical interventions (e.g., hormones, surgery, etc.) to physically change a trans person's body. While there has been a rise of misinformation about gender-affirming medical care, it's important to note that doctors do not perform any gender affirming surgeries on young children, and that any minor receiving gender-affirming medical care is doing so only after extensive evaluation to ensure it is the medically appropriate path.

A **legal transition** consists of changing legal documents (e.g., birth certificate, driver's licenses, etc.) to align with a trans person's gender identity. Educators can generally refer to students by their chosen name and pronouns *without* legal name changes or parental involvement, although this is unfortunately changing as some districts and states implement anti-trans policies and legislation that require teachers and staff to receive parental approval before using a different name for a student, or require the use of a student's legal name.[7]

A Note on Re/Detransition and "What if it's just a phase?"

Some people may **detransition** or **retransition,** which means to cease or change their medical, social, and/or legal transition. Just as transitioning itself is a unique personal experience for each trans person, de/retransitioning is unique to each individual, and the language used around de/retransitioning reflects this. Some people who de/retransition still consider themselves as trans, while others do not. Some people who de/retransition think of their experience as "reversing" or "undoing" some aspect(s) of their transition, while others may not frame their transition as linear and instead experience their re/detransition as simply moving forward with a newer, better understanding of themself.

Many people who may be seen by other people as "detransitioners" cite external factors—such as the cost of transitioning or lack of family support—as part or all of the reason they re/detransition.[8] This raises the question of how much their experience really shares in common with people who realize re/detransitioning is truly right for them, versus those who feel pressured to re/detransition because of social, financial, or other circumstances outside their control.

Unfortunately, the word *detransitioning* has become a particular weapon in passing anti-trans laws and legislation, and discussing de/retransitioning can be an emotionally charged topic. Both the media and anti-trans advocates claim that de/retransitioning is more common than it really is, and the stories of individual people who de/retransition may also be weaponized by these anti-trans advocates to push their policies.

Ultimately, de/retransitioning is quite rare and should be considered as neutrally as any other gender-affirming care. All people should be supported to find a path that is right for them, and supporting individual people who re/detransition should not be used as a justification for blocking access to transition-related care or services for other trans people (see Figure 2.1). Likewise, your job as an educator is to support students where they are right now—which may include things like respecting when a student uses a new name or pronoun—and not second-guess a student or try to predict what might happen in the future.

FIGURE 2.1   Headlines from various articles about de/re-transitioning.[9]

INTERSECTIONALITY: A concept named by Professor Kimberlé Crenshaw in 1989 to describe how various aspects of someone's identity can "intersect" to result in different experiences of discrimination. Over time, the use of the term *intersectionality* has shifted somewhat, from originally referring specifically to how overlapping identities can result in unique types of discrimination to more broadly talking about how over-lapping identities result in unique life experiences in general.

We spoke with Brittni Laura (she/ella), an educator in Colorado who works with A Queer Endeavor, a program at the University of Colorado Boulder School of Education that aims to "make unworkable the silence that historically has surrounded topics of gender and sexual diversity in education." Laura noted that the work of supporting trans students "is inherently intersec-tional" because "there are queer and trans people in all commu-nities. There are queer and trans folks who are neurodivergent, queer and trans folks who are people of color, who fit into all different categories. So, inherently, this work is intersectional. And that means we need a commitment to justice and liberation for all communities."

HETERONORMATIVITY: The expectation, often unspoken, that straight or heterosexual attraction and relationships are "normal" while any other types of attraction and relationships are "abnormal." For example, it is heteronormative to argue that the children's book *Tango Makes Three*—the true story of two male penguins hatching and raising a chick together—is somehow political or inappropriate for children, while classic fairy tales like *Cinderella*, *Sleeping Beauty*, or *Snow White*—all of which involve a young woman falling in love with a male prince—are somehow apolitical or automatically appropriate for children because they only depict heterosexual relationships.

CISNORMATIVITY: The expectation, often unspoken, that cisgender people and bodies are "normal" and transgender people or bodies are "abnormal." For example, it is cisnormative to argue that learning about and respecting people's pronouns is bad or that only trans people care about pronouns because "normal" people don't use them, when, in fact, both cis and trans people use pronouns constantly every day, and learning about pronouns is a foundational component of learning English.

MICROAGGRESSION: A small instance of disrespecting or invalidating someone's identity, whether or not it was done intentionally. Using someone's wrong name or pronouns is a classic example of a microaggression many trans people regularly face. Microaggressions can be like mosquito bites: no one single bite is likely to do permanent damage, but an endless stream of biting and itching can make it absolutely impossible for a student to learn.

MICROAFFIRMATION: A small instance of respecting or validating someone's identity, for example, by using their correct names and pronouns or by ensuring different types of identities are represented in curriculum and classroom materials.

STEALTH: A term describing a trans person who has transitioned and is not out about being trans; being stealth is the opposite of being out. Someone may choose to remain stealth due to concerns around privacy and safety, and it is never appropriate to out someone (or reveal their status as trans) without their knowledge and permission. Adults who are supporting trans students should not assume a student will or won't want to be stealth, and a trans student's feelings about being stealth (or not) may change over time.

GENDER-AFFIRMING CARE: Mental health and medical care that respects and supports someone's gender identity. The U.S. Department of Health and Human Services defines gender-affirming care as "an array of services that may include medical, surgical, mental health, and non-medical services for transgender and nonbinary people."[10] Meanwhile, the World Health Organization defines it as "any single or combination of a number of social, psychological, behavioural [sic], or medical (including hormonal treatment or surgery) interventions designed to support and affirm an individual's gender identity."[11]

CONVERSION THERAPY: A discredited type of therapy that is supposed to "fix" (or "convert") an LGBTQ child or adult into one who is cisgender and heterosexual. This type of treatment can be intensely harmful and distressing, and has no evidence of success. All mainstream health organizations in the United States oppose conversion therapy, including the National Alliance on Mental Illness, the American Academy of Child and Adolescent Psychiatry, the American Academy of Pediatrics, the American Medical Association, and many more. Increasingly, states are passing laws to ban conversion therapy for minors.[12]

GENDER SUPPORT PLAN: A school document outlining a student's understanding of their own gender and identity, the student's family support (or lack thereof), how public or private information about the student's gender will be, and more. For more information, see Chapter 5: Affirm. For a sample gender support plan template, see online version Bonus Resource 4.

NEURODIVERSITY: Harvard Medical School describes neurodiversity as "the idea that people experience and interact with the world around them in many different ways; there is no one 'right' way of thinking, learning, and behaving, and differences are not viewed as deficits." The term was created by Judy Singer in the 1990s as "a political term to argue for the importance of including all neurotypes for a thriving human society," and is strongly associated with the movement for autistic self-advocacy.[13]

While *neurodiversity* is used to describe populations of people, individuals may be described as **neurotypical,** or broadly aligning with how society expects someone to think and interact with the world, or **neurodivergent,** or broadly outside of how society expects someone to think and interact with the world. For more on how and why these concepts connect to supporting trans students, see the section on neurodiversity in Chapter 3.

GROOMING: The past few years has seen a rise in anti-LGBTQ extremists falsely claiming that supporting trans students, learning about LGBTQ identity in school, or even simply acknowledging the existence of LGBTQ people to children, constitutes "grooming."[14] This framing intentionally misrepresents LGBTQ identity, the needs of LGBTQ people, and the importance of learning about diversity and differences while in school.

For context, RAINN (Rape, Abuse & Incest National Network), the largest anti-sexual abuse organization in the United States, defines *grooming* as "manipulative behaviors that the abuser uses to gain access to a potential victim, coerce them to agree to the abuse, and reduce the risk of being caught." The work of supporting trans students is not at all manipulative, coercive, or otherwise abusive.

Conversations within the Trans Community

The trans community is incredibly diverse, with transgender people coming from every race, religion, class, level of ability or disability, immigration status, and every other category that we use to describe populations of people. Trans youth are also not a monolith, and have different wants and needs as well as different opinions about what it means to be trans. As such, not all trans people agree on specific terms and definitions, or even if certain identities should be included within the larger trans community.

As educators and adult allies, it may be appropriate to help trans youth navigate these conversations and disagreements by ensuring that they speak to each other with respect, and to help them do more research or find additional resources when they have questions. At the same time, it is not our role to decide whether or not an individual or a population is "really" trans, or to tell trans youth what language they should or shouldn't use to describe their own identities and experiences.

When it comes to language, here are a few common areas of discussion within the trans community:

Are non-binary people trans? In this book, we use the term *trans* to be inclusive of non-binary people. That said, not all trans people consider non-binary folks to be part of the trans community, and not all non-binary people consider themselves to be trans. We include non-binary under the trans umbrella because, as noted elsewhere, trans and non-binary students face similar obstacles in school and require similar support from educators and other adults.

(Continued)

(Continued)

Are intersex people trans? Not all intersex people are trans. However, according to interACT, an organization that advocates on behalf of intersex youth, "intersex and transgender people both challenge the common myth that gender is dependent on body parts. The two communities face many overlapping issues. Often, transgender people have to fight to access surgeries that they do want, while intersex people have to fight against surgeries that they don't want—or already received as young children without their consent."[15]

Should trans identity be medicalized? Transgender identity has historically been included in the *Diagnostic and Statistical Manual of Mental Disorders* (*DSM*), an extensive list of what the American Psychiatric Association considers to be diagnosable conditions. On the one hand, trans people may need to receive a diagnosis before being allowed to access gender-affirming services or healthcare, and a diagnosis may be required by insurance before that care is covered. On the other hand, many trans activists and advocates argue that being trans is not a mental health condition and should not be included in the *DSM*, similar to how "homosexuality" was once included in the *DSM* but was removed in 1973. While being trans is no longer considered a medical disorder in and of itself, the *DSM V*, released in 2013, contains the diagnosis of "gender dysphoria," replacing the earlier "gender identity disorder," which itself replaced the "transsexualism."

Given the state of insurance and healthcare in the United States, it is unlikely that trans identity will be removed from the *DSM* anytime soon, but this is an ongoing topic of discussion among many trans advocates and medical providers.

Is being transgender a disability? Similar to the question of whether or not trans identity should be medicalized, there is also discussion within the trans community about whether or not gender dysphoria should be classified as a disability. This is both a political and a practical question, as the Americans with Disabilities Act of 1990, commonly known as the ADA, offers significant protections to students to ensure that students with disabilities have equal access to educational spaces and opportunities; as such, the ADA could potentially be used as a tool to advocate for the needs of trans and non-binary students.

Whether or not gender dysphoria meets the legal definition of a disability is somewhat unclear, as the ADA did not create a checklist of approved or legally-recognized disabilities. Instead, the Act defines an individual with a disability as "a person who has a physical or mental impairment that substantially limits one or more major life activities, a person who has a history or record of such an impairment, or a person who is perceived by others as having such an impairment." Further complicating things, the actual language of the ADA specifically excludes "gender identity disorders not resulting from physical impairments," but in 2022, a federal court found that gender dysphoria *could* be covered by the ADA under some circumstances.[16]

Disability rights activist and "all around general troublemaker" Rebecca Cokley (she/her) said this discussion connects to decades of conversations within disability advocacy spaces:

> I remember in the late '80s, early '90s, around the time the ADA passed, [trans] people being very adamant and saying, "No, we're not disabled.
>
> "What I believe has come to pass from the disability space is that as we've moved from disability being pursued as a medical construct—the idea that people with disabilities are broken, and that it's on the benevolence of non-disabled people to fix us—to a broader conversation around the social model of disability, which is it's not that we're broken, it's that society is broken and we collectively have a responsibility to make a society more inclusive of all people, including people with disabilities. And we know that, by making society more physically and socially accessible for disabled people, we make it more physically and socially accessible for everybody.
>
> "As the understanding has moved in that direction, I have heard from trans friends and chosen family that there

(Continued)

(*Continued*)

has been more of an interest in making the argument about gender dysphoria as a disability because with it comes the access to accommodations under law. It also comes with Title III protections, which are: access to public accommodations, access to banking, access to grocery stores, etc."

Cokley also noted that the question of whether or not gender dysphoria should be considered a disability is something of a "third rail conversation": it connects to personal identity, political and legal strategy, intersectional and cross-community experiences, and deep-seated emotions people have about what it means to be labeled as disabled. This book does not attempt to answer the question of whether or not gender dysphoria should be considered a disability under the ADA.

Putting It into Practice

Following are scenarios to consider about addressing real-world challenges and personal reflection questions to ask yourself. We encourage you to take some time to reflect and catch your breath before taking action.

Personal Reflection Questions

1. Which of the terms in this chapter resonates with your understanding of yourself? Why?
2. Did any of the information in this chapter prompt you to think about your own identity differently? If so, why?

Addressing Real-World Challenges

1. Language around trans and non-binary identities are, like all language, evolving. How could you ensure you are using the most up-to-date and affirming language in your setting?

2. Let's say you hear a colleague using an out-of-date term like *hermaphrodite*. How do you handle the situation?

3. Two students are arguing over the definition of the word *queer*. What input could you provide, and how might you help facilitate the conversation?

Notes

1. For a guided exploration through your own gender journey, intended specifically for adults who work with families and children, visit https://www.tfaforms.com/4777837.

2. "Non-binary," LGBTQIA+ Wiki, n.d. (accessed May 29, 2023), https://lgbtqia.fandom.com/wiki/LGBTQIA%2B_Wiki. Note: LGBTQIA+ Wiki is a "dedicated resource for LGBTQIA+ topics, including sexual and romantic orientations, gender identities, and the LGBTQIA+ community as a whole."

3. Garima Garg, Ghada Elshimy, and Raman Marwaha, *Gender Dysphoria* (Treasure Island, FL: StatPearls Publishing, 2022); and StatPearls (Internet), last updated October 16, 2022, https://www.ncbi.nlm.nih.gov/books/NBK532313/.

4. Juliette Rocheleau, "A former slur is reclaimed, and listeners have mixed feelings," *NPR*, August 21, 2019, https://www.npr.org/sections/publiceditor/2019/08/21/752330316/a-former-slur-is-reclaimed-and-listeners-have-mixed-feelings.

5. "Pronouns," *The Chicago Manual of Style Online*, n.d., https://www.chicagomanualofstyle.org/qanda/data/faq/topics/Pronouns/faq0031.html; citing "A note on the nonbinary 'they': It's now in the dictionary," *Merriam-Webster*, September 19, 2019, https://www.merriam-webster.com/words-at-play/nonbinary-they-is-in-the-dictionary; "Singular 'they': Though singular 'they' is old, 'they' as a nonbinary pronoun is new—and useful," *Merriam-Webster*, September 2019, https://www.merriam-webster.com/words-at-play/singular-nonbinary-they; Dennis Baron, "A brief history of singular 'they,'" *Oxford English Dictionary*, September

4, 2018, https://public.oed.com/blog/a-brief-history-of-singular-they/; Lauren Easton, "Making a case for a singular 'they,'" *AP Blog*, March 24, 2017, https://blog.ap.org/products-and-services/making-a-case-for-a-singular-they.

6. For more on neopronouns, see HRC's explainer at "Understanding neopronouns," Human Rights Campaign Foundation, last updated May 18, 2022, https://www.hrc.org/resources/understanding-neopronouns.

7. Alec Johnson, "Arrowhead students must have parental permission to use different names and pronouns at school, new policy says," *Milwaukee Journal Sentinel*, updated September 16, 2022, https://www.jsonline.com/story/communities/lake-country/news/hartland/2022/09/16/arrowhead-students-need-parental-permission-change-names-pronouns/10378343002/; Kerry Sheridan, "Students who want to change their name or pronouns in Sarasota schools must now get parental permission," *WUSF Public Media*—WUSF 89.7 August 16, 2022, https://wusfnews.wusf.usf.edu/education/2022-08-16/students-who-want-to-change-their-name-or-pronouns-in-sarasota-schools-must-now-get-parental-permission.

8. Jack L. Turban, Stephanie S. Loo, Anthony N. Almazan, and Alex S. Keuroghlian, "Factors leading to 'detransition' among transgender and gender diverse people in the United States: A mixed-methods analysis," *LGBT Health* 8, no. 4 (June 1, 2021): 273–280, https://doi.org/10.1089/lgbt.2020.0437.

9. De/re-transition choices., https://slate.com/human-interest/2023/01/trans-detransition-facts-research-study-atlantic.html; https://www.newsweek.com/what-data-shows-about-transgender-detransition-regret-1807448; https://www.huckmag.com/article/debunking-the-dangerous-myths-around-detransition; https://apnews.com/article/transgender-treatment-regret-detransition-371e927ec6e7a24cd9c77b5371c6ba2b; https://www.vice.com/en/article/m7bjvq/south-dakota-forced-detransitioning; https://www.nytimes.com/2023/05/16/us/politics/transgender-care-detransitioners.html.

10. "Gender-affirming care and young people," OAHS, Office of Population Affairs, HHS, March 2022, https://opa.hhs.gov/sites/default/files/2022-03/gender-affirming-care-young-people-march-2022.pdf.

11. "Gender incongruence and transgender health in the ICD," World Health Organization, n.d., https://www.who.int/standards/classifications/frequently-asked-questions/gender-incongruence-and-transgender-health-in-the-icd.

12. "Conversion therapy," National Alliance on Mental Illness, n.d., https://www.nami.org/Advocacy/Policy-Priorities/Stopping-Harmful-Practices/Conversion-Therapy; "Conversion therapy," American Academy of Child and Adolescent Psychiatry, February 2018, https://www.aacap.org/aacap/Policy_Statements/2018/Conversion_Therapy.aspx; Committee on Adolescence, "Homosexuality and adolescence," *Pediatrics* 92, no. 4 (October 1993): 631–634, American Academy of Pediatrics, https://doi.org/10.1542/peds.92.4.631; "Sexual orientation and gender identity change efforts (so-called 'conversion therapy')," American Medical Association and GLMA, n.d., https://www.ama-assn.org/system/files/conversion-therapy-issue-brief.pdf; "Policy and position statements on conversion therapy," Human Rights Campaign, n.d., https://www.hrc.org/resources/policy-and-position-statements-on-conversion-therapy; "Equality maps: Conversion therapy laws," Movement Advancement Project, n.d., https://www.lgbtmap.org/equality-maps/conversion_therapy.

13. Nicole Baumer and Julia Frueh, "What is neurodiversity?" Harvard Health Publishing, Harvard Medical School, November 23, 2021, https://www.health.harvard.edu/blog/what-is-neurodiversity-202111232645; Judy Singer, "Neurodiversity: Definition and discussion," *Reflections on Neurodiversity,* June 2019, https://neurodiversity2.blogspot.com/p/what.html.

14. Center on Extremism, "What is 'grooming?' The truth behind the dangerous, bigoted lie targeting the LGBTQ+ community," Anti-Defamation League, September 16, 2022, https://www.adl.org/resources/blog/what-grooming-truth-behind-dangerous-bigoted-lie-targeting-lgbtq-community.

15. "FAQ: Intersex, gender, and LGBTQIA+," InterAct Advocates for Intersex Youth, last updated May 18, 2020, https://interact advocates.org/faq/intersex-lgbtqia/.

16. Rebecca Leaf, "Gender dysphoria recognized as a disability under federal law," Miles & Stockbridge *MSLaw Blog*, August 19, 2022, https://www.mslaw.com/mslaw-blog/gender-dysphoria-recognized-as-a-disability-under-federal-law.

CHAPTER THREE

Supporting Diverse Student Bodies

"Public school design in this country, and the practices that most of us employ based on traditional morality and religious values, mean children who are Black, Latinx, Native, disabled, presumed to be queer, or who don't affirm people's expectations around gender roles or presentation, are seldom acknowledged as human, and they don't get any kind of love."

—Dr. David J. Johns (he/him), Executive Director
of the National Black Justice Coalition

IT'S IMPORTANT to remember that trans youth in schools are, first and foremost, like any other group of students: they need supportive teachers, inclusive learning environments, a range of extracurricular activities, opportunities to make friends, and help navigating the difficult journey from childhood to adulthood. In most instances, trans students have more in common with their cis peers than not, and teachers should ask the same questions about trans students that they ask about any students: Do they understand the material? Do they have the knowledge and support needed to complete their assignments? Is there anything happening outside of class that might be making it more difficult for them to learn?

Similarly, trans students have the same rights as any other student to not be the target of bullying or gossip, to have their privacy respected, and to be physically and emotionally safe at school.

As we will touch on again and again, the adults working with trans students—teachers, school librarians, school counselors, and school administrators—already have many of the tools they need to ensure their trans students are happy and thriving because they're the same tools they're already using with cis students. Nevertheless, it's worth noting some areas where trans students may encounter extra friction or need additional support when compared to their cis peers.

Educators must also remember that trans students come from all races, classes, religions, family structures, and more. Trans students have different abilities and come in all shapes and sizes. Focusing on a certain type of trans person, or assuming all trans students come from a particular race or socioeconomic background, means that you will inevitably be leaving out trans students who don't conform to those expectations. Teachers who make that mistake will fall short celebrating the beautiful diversity that exists within the trans community (and, indeed, in every community).

Race and Racism

By every available metric, trans people of color (sometimes abbreviated to TPOC) face more obstacles and more discrimination in the United States than their white trans peers. These experiences are often even worse for trans women of color, and especially for Black trans women.[1] Similarly, readers of this book are likely familiar with the many education disparities that exist in American schools, particularly when it comes to race and class.

It should come as no surprise, then, that transgender students of color do not always feel supported in school, even in classrooms or districts where educators are actively trying to support and affirm trans youth. For example, the Trevor Project's 2022 *National Survey on LGBTQ Youth Mental Health* found that LGBTQ youth of color were generally more likely than their white peers to have considered or attempted suicide in the last year.[2]

Dr. David J. Johns, the Executive Director of the National Black Justice Coalition (NBJC), highlighted this racial disparity when we spoke with him, explaining that "too often, education research ignores the intersectional identities of Black Queer students, focusing instead and often superficially on Black students (assumed to be cisgender and heterosexual) or Queer students," assumed to be white. This means that "children who are members of multiple marginalized communities are not only erased and rendered invisible in schools, but in that process, they also face additional, sometimes indescribable challenges."

To put it bluntly, not all trans students are white and not all students of color are cis or straight.

Trans Joy

[Trans joy] reminds me of Black joy. You know, being a Black person myself with all the Black boy magic, Black girl magic and Black boy joy, all of that. It just speaks of like a pride in who you are and things that you can't change about yourself.

—Ny'Jal Lyons (he/him)[3]

Issues of race and racism are also directly connected to book bans, curriculum restrictions, and the increasing number of objections to so-called "critical race theory" (CRT) being taught to K–12 students. These bans and restrictions intentionally make it difficult to talk about past and present experiences of discrimination, with one proposed Florida law going so far as to require that schools teach about slavery, oppression, and discrimination without causing any students "discomfort, guilt, anguish, or any other form of psychological distress on account of his or her race."[4] While students certainly shouldn't be made to feel guilt or anguish over historical wrongdoings, it is wildly unrealistic to expect that students can learn about and discuss difficult topics like slavery without ever feeling any discomfort.

At their core, curriculum restrictions and book bans are about placing the comfort of some students over ensuring that *all* students learn about the (sometimes uncomfortable) realities of both history and of the present day. Supporting all trans students requires acknowledging and addressing issues of racism that exist in your education community.

Physical Disabilities

As transgender students come from all communities and backgrounds, disabled trans students often require the same support needed by their disabled cis peers.[5] To learn more about disability advocacy and how to best support disabled students, we spoke with Rebecca Cokley, a disability rights activist and self-described "all around general troublemaker." Cokley served as the executive director of the National Council on Disability during the Obama Administration and is currently the first U.S. Disability Rights Program Officer for the Ford Foundation.

We asked Cokley about the connections between disability rights and trans rights, and she found parallels between the ways trans people and disabled people are rejected by family members, and the similar needs in each community to push for the right and ability to access public spaces:

> All forms of oppression come from the same tree.
> They may manifest differently, but they all show
> up very similarly. What I found from my time
> with NCTE [the National Center for Transgender
> Equality], and NBJC [the National Black Justice
> Coalition], was that my husband and I found our-
> selves spending a lot of time in trans-centering spaces.
> He and I have ended up with a whole cadre of young
> people that we have sort of mentored and raised up
> over the years being chosen family, young people who
> were ostracized by their families for either being trans

> or disabled or both. And so we as a family feel very
> strong about showing up in solidarity.
>
> And for the trans community and the disability
> community, a lot of it [advocacy] has been how do
> we obtain public access? And how do we maintain it?
> Whether it's the right to go to schools and be safe, to
> be in an inclusive learning environment, and to see
> ourselves represented in the curriculum. To having
> bathrooms that worked for us. There are so many par-
> allels across our movements in terms of public access
> and what it means.

When it comes to supporting disabled trans students, Cokley identified both IEPs (Individualized Education Programs) and 504 Plans as potentially important tools; 504 Plans are called that because they refer to Section 504 of the Rehabilitation Act of 1973, which "protects qualified individuals from discrimination based on their disability."[6] Federal law does not require a medical diagnosis to implement a 504 Plan, although a medical diagnosis can be taken into consideration when a school evaluates a student for a potential 504 Plan. That said, state or local laws may have additional conditions related to 504 Plans, and may require a medical diagnosis. As always, it's a good idea to research your state and local laws committing to a specific course of action.

While IEPs and 504 Plans can have similar content, 504 Plans are generally less detailed than IEPs and more broadly focus on how to remove barriers for a student who does not need personalized instruction. For more information on IEPs, see Chapter 5: Affirm. Cokley described 504 plans this way:

> The easiest way to think about it is that physical access
> to facilities is a 504 plan. Adaptations to curriculum
> and instruction is an IEP. My kids have a 504 plan,
> because we haven't had to modify their access to the
> curriculum at all. And so with a 504 plan, it means
> my kids—who are short statured—have step stools in

every classroom, lowered paper towel dispensers in the
bathroom, step stools in the bathroom, conversations
around how their schedule is structured so that they're
not going from one side of the school building to
the other side of the school building. If they need
a second set of books, that is all covered under that
[504 plan].

For a disabled trans student, 504 plan might ensure that the
student doesn't need to trek all the way across school to access
the only available gender-neutral bathroom, or has extra physical
space and privacy while changing for gym.

Above all, Cokley emphasized the need to support "the
whole student":

What are all the different pieces that the student
brings to the table? What are all the different identities they bring to the table? It's doing the research. If
you learn that a student who's trans also has ADHD,
do your ADHD homework. And be mindful to not
always say that cohabitating is comorbidity. Just as
like we see it in the disability space, where a school, if
they have a student who is Deaf and depressed, will
say, "Well, of course, they're depressed, they're Deaf!" I
could easily see a school saying, "Well, of course, that
student is depressed, they're trans!" And they may be
related, or they might not. And so actually taking the
time to do not what's necessarily easiest, in terms of
bureaucracy and paperwork, but actually getting to
know the student and getting to know what they're
dealing with.

There's a lot of joy and beauty in the trans
disability connection. For two communities that have
historically been subjected to such violence, trauma,
eradication, the fact that we're still here is a testament
to our power, to our communities, the work of our

elders, the gains of our descendants. We're strong and we're vulnerable. We hold the possible. Nothing is more beautiful than seeing a trans kid see themselves as beautiful, a disabled kid see themselves as beautiful, and recognizing beauty in their community.

Neurodiversity

There is growing evidence both that transgender people are more likely to be autistic, and that autistic people are more likely to identify as LGBTQ.[7] We spoke with Finn V. Gratton (they/them), a somatic psychotherapist and author of the book *Supporting Transgender Autistic Youth and Adults*, about the need to consider autism specifically, and neurodiversity more broadly, when supporting trans students:[8]

> There's the surface level [justification], which is that the current number is 11% of trans folks are also autistic.[9] So, in that, of course it's an intersectional issue. You can't do trans support without being aware of trans autistic experience. In a deeper, more fundamental way, they're [trans identity and neurodiversity] not completely separate experiences. When I ask at an autism training for people to think of an early time when they first remember being made "wrong," in the way of, "I was just being me, and all of a sudden somebody's made me wrong, and even punished or rejected me for it," they come up with gender policing, or experiences when somebody said, "that's not what boys do, or that's not what girls do. You can't do that."
>
> So both gender and other behaviors are heavily policed by a neuro-normative, heteronormative, gender-normative, binary-normative system. So, just

by recognizing and expressing our trans or non-binary identities, we've stepped out of neuro-normativity, because neuro-normativity sets up the whole idea of male brain, female brain, masculinity and femininity. So anyone who does that—whether they are trans or gender non-conforming in other ways—is taking a step outside of neuro-normative and toward neurodivergent embodiment.

How the two [trans and neurodivergent experience and expression] are treated in society is different, but they're both queering the experience of being human. It's a fundamental self-authoring of the truth of one's own experience, over the force of normative pressures. Nick Walker in *Neuroqueer Heresies* and Remi Yergeau in *Authoring Autism*, go into much more detail about neuroqueering.

Gratton also cautioned about the potential dangers of attempting to explain why such an overlap exists between trans and neurodiverse communities, particularly in an education environment. First, trans people and neurodivergent people *do* exist, so a parent or educator focusing on "why" may be distracted from the actual needs of that specific student. Educators are not responsible for diagnosing or treating the physical or mental health conditions of their students, and should not attempt to rationalize or explain why any particular student is (or isn't) transgender.

Gratton also noted that some people may use a trans person's neurodivergence as justification for why that person can't "really" be trans:

We're asking the wrong question when we ask, "Why are autistic people like that?" We don't know why about a whole lot of things. People *are* trans. I believe people keep asking the why question because they see deviance in both autism and trans experiences and are trying to explain one deviance by the other deviance.

Turn it around: Why are so many neurotypical people also cis and hetrosexual?

The "why" question is a problem because anti-trans folks are really grabbing onto it. They're saying, "Oh, these autistic people, they must not be trans because they don't really understand gender, or because they're trying to fit in with some social thing." They're using biases and ignorance around autism and around trans experiences to create false explanations for the higher incidence of autistic people within the trans population.

And that is affecting services. Parents or guardians may say, "I'm afraid my autistic child isn't fully understanding their experience or choices; therefore we cannot consent to, or need to put the brakes on, their social or medical transition." It's the job of care providers, along with the individual and the guardians of all trans and non-binary individuals, to support understanding of medical transition choices and effects and to identify capacity to make informed consent, whether the individual is autistic or not. Many of my autistic clients come in with lots of research and understanding of transition choices and impacts; some have less understanding. Just as with all my clients, I will spend time helping them gather enough information and understanding to make choices for their well-being. Sadly, there's word out in the trans autistic community: "don't get assessed or diagnosed [as autistic] before you get your medical transition, because somebody might get in the way." This reminds me of how trans people of an earlier generation pretended to be heterosexual and binary gendered, when many weren't, so that they could get the medical transition care they needed.

To ensure education environments support neurodivergent students, Gratton says schools should include neurodivergent voices and consider neurodiversity "from the beginning":

> A challenging aspect of inclusion is that there's so much range to neurodivergence, both in ability and in intersectional experiences. Schools need to consider how they communicate about gender, in implicit and explicit ways in both mainstream and special education settings. This includes how we communicate about gender and sexuality with non-speaking and intellectually disabled students. What do social pragmatics groups and classes around living skills reinforce or disrupt around normed gender identities and roles?
>
> BIPOC students often are misdiagnosed with oppositional defiant disorder or conduct disorder, leading to the special-ed-to-prison pipeline. It is our BIPOC trans/non-binary and autistic students who are most in need of attention and advocacy to reduce trauma associated with punishment, discrimination, exclusion, and lack of support.[10]
>
> There needs to be education for everyone—students, guardians, and school staff—around different cognitive, sensory, and speaking processes. People need to understand that different types of processing and different communication styles are not "wrong," even if these differences make you uncomfortable or confused. Just as with every other form of diversity in our world, the real work is with everyone appreciating diversity and recognizing the ways normative structures hurt minority groups, in this case neuro and gender minorities. [See Figure 3.1.]

ASAN Condemns Restrictions on Gender-Affirming Care

'Significant Overlap': Researchers Work to Understand Connection Between Autism and Gender Fluidity

Trans People's Mental Health Is Being Weaponized Against Them

Transgender and nonbinary people are up to six times more likely to have autism

Autistic LGBTQ community seeks louder voice in debate

Georgia's new anti-trans law also disparages autistic people like me

FIGURE 3.1   A selection of headlines about potential links between neurodiversity and trans identity.[11]

Economic Class

Sometimes, supporting a transgender student may cost nothing: referring to someone using the correct name and pronouns, for example, does not require a financial investment. That said, some aspects of transitioning may cost money, including medical fees (not always covered by insurance), legal fees (in some states, a legal name change costs hundreds of dollars), or simply the cost of buying a new wardrobe.

A huge portion of teenagers in the United States—roughly one third—live in ZIP codes classified by the U.S. Census Bureau as concentrated poverty areas, and well over half of all youth of color live in such high-poverty areas, meaning these costs may be out of their reach.[12]

We asked TC Caldwell (they/them), the Community Engagement Director at the Knights and Orchids Society (TKO), about how race and class can impact the experiences of trans students. TKO's mission is "to help more Black trans, same-gender-loving, and Black queer folks access high-quality primary care and endocrinology services."[13] Caldwell explained:

> Non-white parents and lower middle income families often don't have the time, energy or financial resources to invest into making sure that their child is in a school where they are being treated fairly. Needing to work long hours, navigating racism, and prioritizing survival often hinders parents from being able to fully show up for their trans children. Unfortunately, those children are often in schools that don't even know or care where to begin when it comes to affirming and supporting trans students.

When supporting trans students, it's important to keep in mind what financial resources they may (or may not) have access to and, where possible, offer alternative resources or support structures. For example, suggesting a trans student check out the local thrift store may be helpful advice, or perhaps the school's GSA could organize a free clothing swap. Likewise, there are a number of organizations that offer free chest binders for trans youth including Point of Pride, the American Trans Resource Hub, B4CK (Binders for Confident Youth), and more. Likewise, local LGBTQ community centers or health centers may have resources to help trans people access gender-affirming care, while LGBTQ advocacy orgs may have name-change clinics or grants to help trans and non-binary folks legally change their documents.

Family Structure and Dynamics

Any student's education can be complicated by family structure or dynamics, and trans students are no different. Some trans students are loved and affirmed by both their immediate and extended family. The families of some trans students require their own journey and learning before coming to understand the importance of supporting their trans child. And, unfortunately, some family members may never be supportive.

Similarly, it's possible that one parent will support their trans child while another parent will not. There is no easy way to navigate this type of tricky situation, other than to ensure that the trans student's needs are being placed first.

It's also possible that a trans student's family structures and dynamics may be weighing on that student's mind, but not for anything having to do with being trans—maybe the student's parents just got divorced, maybe there was a death in the family, or maybe a sibling's needs mean the parents have less time to focus on that trans student.

Finally, a trans student may have a parent or family member who is also part of the LGBTQ community. These families may still want or need help supporting their trans child, as being LGBTQ does not mean someone will automatically know what to do.

Organizations that support families with trans kids include PFLAG, the Trans Youth Equality Foundation, TransFamilies, Stand with Trans, Gender Spectrum, HRC's Parents for Transgender Equality National Council, Trans Youth Family Allies, and more.

Putting It into Practice

Following are scenarios to consider about addressing real-world challenges and personal reflection questions to ask yourself. We encourage you to take some time to reflect and catch your breath before taking action.

Personal Reflection Questions

1. What intersecting identities do you see present in students in your setting?
2. Which identities are focused on in professional development (PD) and which are not?
3. Why do you think that is?
4. When have you felt supported in all aspects of who you are?
5. What did that support feel like?
6. When have you not felt supported in all aspects of who you are?
7. What did that lack of support feel like?

Addressing Real-World Challenges

1. No two students are exactly alike, and students may come from backgrounds that are very different from your own. How should educators approach this reality, and what can educators do to best support every single student?
2. What other issues might trans students in your community be facing? How can you ensure that the support you offer is mindful of those issues?
3. Given your current role and situation, what real-world challenges does this section bring up for you in your community? How might you approach those challenges? What resources currently exist from your school/district/board of education to handle these challenges?

4. If your current role changed, how might your thoughts on these challenges change? Think about how you might answer differently as a classroom teacher, a school principal, a district administrator, and so on.

Notes

1. Kali Cyrus, "Multiple minorities as multiply marginalized: Applying the minority stress theory to LGBTQ people of color," *Journal of Gay & Lesbian Mental Health* 21, no. 3 (2017): 194–202, https://doi.org/10.1080/19359705.2017.1320739; Kevin Jefferson, Torsten B. Neilands, and Jae Sevelius, "Transgender women of color: Discrimination and depression symptoms," *Ethnicity and Inequalities in Health and Social Care* 6, no. 4 (2013): 121–136, https://doi.org/10.1108/EIHSC-08-2013-0013; Annamarie Forestiere, "America's war on Black trans women," *Harvard Civil Rights—Civil Liberties Law Review*, September 23, 2020, https://harvardcrcl.org/americas-war-on-black-trans-women/.

2. The Trevor Project, *2022 National Survey on LGBTQ Youth Mental Health*, n.d., https://www.thetrevorproject.org/survey-2022/.

3. Ny'Jal Lyons, quoted in Daylina Miller, "Trans joy: Black joy and family acceptance," *WUSF Public Media—WUSF 89.7*, June 22, 2022, https://wusfnews.wusf.usf.edu/local-state/2022-06-22/trans-joy-black-joy-family-acceptance.

4. Ivory A. Toldson, "New study reveals the anti-CRT agenda is really about denying racism and revising history," *Diverse: Issues in Higher Education*, October 25, 2022, https://www.diverseeducation.com/opinion/article/15302120/new-study-reveals-the-anticrt-agenda-is-really-about-denying-racism-and-revising-history; The Professional Staff of the Committee on Education, "SB 148 Bill Analysis and Financial Impact Statement," Florida Senate, January 2022, https://www.flsenate.gov/Session/Bill/2022/148/Analyses/2022s00148.pre.ed.PDF.

5.   There are ongoing conversations within disabled communities about using people-first language (e.g., "people with disabilities") versus identity-first language (e.g., "disabled people"). Rebecca Cockley said she "goes back and forth all the time," but she generally used identity-first language during our interview. With that in mind, we use identify-first language in this section but we strongly encourage you to speak with disabled members of your education community to see what language they use and prefer, and why.

6.   "Your Rights Under Section 504 of the Rehabilitation Act" Fact Sheet, U.S. Department of Health and Human Services Office for Civil Rights, revised June 2006, https://www.hhs.gov/sites/default/files/ocr/civilrights/resources/factsheets/504.pdf.

7.   Varun Warrier, David M. Greenberg, Elizabeth Weir, Clara Buckingham, Paula Smith, Meng-Chuan Lai, Carrie Allison, and Simon Baron-Cohen, "Elevated rates of autism, other neurodevelopmental and psychiatric diagnoses, and autistic traits in transgender and gender-diverse individuals," *Nature Communications* 11, no. 1 (August 7, 2020): 3959, https://doi.org/10.1038/s41467-020-17794-1; "Autistic individuals are more likely to be LGBTQ+," University of Cambridge, September 20, 2021, https://www.cam.ac.uk/research/news/autistic-individuals-are-more-likely-to-be-lgbtq, citing Elizabeth Weir, Carrie Allison, and Simon Baron-Cohen, "The sexual health, orientation, and activity of autistic adolescents and adults," *Autism Research* 14, no. 11 (November 2021): 2342–2354, https://doi.org/10.1002/aur.2604.

8.   Like with the language around physical disability, there are ongoing conversations within neurodiverse communities about using people-first language (e.g., "people with autism" or "people with neurodivergences") versus identity-first language (e.g., "autistic people" or "neurodivergent people"). Gratton strongly preferred identity-first language, which is why we use it in this section.

9.   Aimilia Kallitsounaki and David M. Williams, "Autism Spectrum Disorder and Gender Dysphoria/Incongruence. A Systematic Literature Review and Meta-Analysis," *Journal of*

Autism and Developmental Disorders, May 20, 2022, https://doi .org/10.1007/s10803-022-05517-y.

10. David S. Mandell, Richard F. Ittenbach, Susan E. Levy, and Jennifer A. Pinto-Martin, "Disparities in diagnoses received prior to a diagnosis of autism spectrum disorder," *Journal of Autism and Developmental Disorders* 37, no. 9 (October 2007): 1795–1802, https:// doi.org/10.1007/s10803-006-0314-8.

11. https://www.npr.org/2023/01/15/1149318664/transgender-and-non-binary-people-are-up-to-six-times-more-likely-to-have-au tism; https://www.msnbc.com/opinion/msnbc-opinion/georgias-new-anti-trans-law-also-disparages-autistic-people-rcna76858; https://thehill.com/homenews/lgbtq/4069745-autistic-lgbtq-community-seeks-louder-voice-in-debate/; https://www.kqed.org/ news/11937857/significant-overlap-researchers-work-to-understand-connection-between-autism-and-gender-fluidity; https://www.wired.com/story/trans-gender-affirming-care-mental-health-autism/; https://autisticadvocacy.org/2023/03/asan-condemns-restrictions-on-gender-affirming-care/.

12. Michael Sadowski, *Safe Is Not Enough: Better Schools for LGBTQ Students,* Youth Development and Education Series (Cambridge, MA: Harvard Education Press, 2016), p. 67.

13. "Our Story," The Knights and Orchids Society, n.d., https://www .tkosociety.org/about.

The Four Core
Principles

CHAPTER FOUR

Educate

"If we want to have teachers who reflect the kind of gender expansiveness that at least I envision for schools, then we need to have our teacher education programs also be safer spaces. And right now they're not."

—Dr. Melinda Mangin (she/her)

PERHAPS THE most foundational thing you can do to support trans and non-binary students is educate the adults who work with them. It is critical to provide teachers, administrators, and school staff with the knowledge and tools they need to support trans and non-binary students, and to ensure that education is ongoing and reflects the needs of your particular community.

All educators approach their work with life experiences, belief systems, and skills that make them as diverse as the students they serve. Many teachers follow traditional paths to become educators, through undergrad and graduate programs—while others take non-traditional routes, or become teachers later in life. Whatever route brought you to working with students, it's possible that you did not receive adequate professional development (PD) around supporting LGBTQ students in general and transgender and non-binary students in particular.

This lack of knowledge about the needs of trans and non-binary students makes it doubly important that schools proactively educate their staff, and not simply assume that staff will have the information they need to create truly inclusive learning environments. Likewise, this education should be offered in a non-confrontational manner, with enough time and space for processing and discussing what is learned. Ultimately, requiring teachers to support trans and non-binary students may push some teachers outside of their comfort zone. While this is unavoidable, it should still be done with as much care and thoughtfulness as possible.

We must also remember that out trans students are not the only trans people in school communities. In addition to students who may not be out as trans, cis students may have trans friends and family members, or there may be trans staff. PD should be mindful of these realities; it's wise to always assume that not everyone in a school community is cisgender.

Proactively educating school staff is particularly important because, right now, many educators only think about the needs of trans and non-binary students when faced with the first out trans or non-binary student in their class. This often results in an unfair expectation that those trans students take the lead on educating not only their classmates but their teachers as well. While teachers are always learning from their students, those students should not be expected or relied on to teach adults about the needs of specific student populations.

As trans student Stella Keating (she/her) shared, "Having my teacher essentially ask me to do the curriculum [about trans identity] for her because she didn't want to get it wrong made me really upset because it's not my job on two levels. One, it isn't my job because I'm your student. Secondly, it's not my job because my life isn't educating everyone on being transgender."

Determining Who to Train

A veteran principal once said that the most important members of his team were the cafeteria staff, janitorial staff, and front office staff. Why? Because they interact with everyone!

Our culture commonly talks about classroom teachers as having the most impact on student experience, but many of the adults who work with students are not classroom teachers. Those adults may also have eyes on the community—and on students—in ways teachers don't. For example, someone who works in the cafeteria may be the first to recognize signs of food insecurity. A front-office member who works closely with student records and families may be the first to notice patterns in student absences. Janitorial staff enter all classrooms, and are often in shared spaces and bathrooms; they may see behaviors that classroom teachers do not. Likewise, all staff have opportunities to interact with students, and staff support (or lack of support) can make all the difference in a trans student's life. (See Figure 4.1.)

But how often are these important members of the school community integrated into PD? Not often enough. And when it comes to transgender students and their safety and well-being in school, having eyes on students from these critical perspectives—and in these common spaces—is integral to ensuring student safety.

So what is the pathway to ensuring your *full* staff have what they need to support the growing number of transgender and non-binary students in our schools?

First, you'll want to identify all the personnel who should receive this training. (Remember: think beyond classroom teachers!) List out everyone who makes up your school community as well as in what ways they interact with students. For each role, identify why training on supporting transgender students would be relevant to their work and to student safety and success.

Next consider the logistics of PD opportunities to ensure easy and open access, including:

- When in the school year does the PD take place? What time and what day of the week?
- Where is it held? Is the space physically accessible to all?

Thank You My Allies

When you call me by the name and pronouns I adore, you give me

a gentle warm hug

a hand up

a healing balm

a bright smile in the dark

a heart opening wink

a bouquet of Sunflowers

a Yarrow blossom circle of protection

a tender Rose of sweetness

years on my life

a burst of energy

the ability to focus

a nourishing sense of safety and belonging

a happy memory

a warm cup of Lemon Balm love

When you call me by the name and pronouns I adore, you give me wellness, welcome and home

Thank you

FIGURE 4.1   Keath Silva, Thank You My Allies, 2021.[1]

- In what languages are resources provided?
- Who pays for the training?
- Is the training mandatory? Why or why not?
- What if someone can't attend?

It's also important to communicate the need for, and goal(s) of, the PD session(s), to encourage buy-in from both staff and community members. For more on why this work is important, see "Focusing on Trans and Non-Binary Students" in the Introduction.

We spoke with Booker Marshall at Chicago Public Schools about the push from district leadership to require training for all district staff:

> In 2020, [Chicago Public Schools] rolled out the first mandatory training on supporting transgender and gender non-conforming students. And this was, in part, because a leader in the district, Chief Education Officer LaTanya McDade, came to a training that we had at our Summer Leadership Institute, which is PD for principals. She is a beautiful example of a leader really reflecting on an experience she had as a principal [concerning a transgender student] where things could have been handled differently. And she was like, everybody should be taking this training.
>
> Since then, that training has grown. It was like a quick and dirty 30 minutes of how you have to meet these guidelines [on supporting trans students] and what the protections are. And now it's how to interpret the law, what you need to do to follow the law, but it also goes much deeper than the law.
>
> We now have it in webinar format. Because of the scale of our district—we have over 41,000 staff—it's not feasible to do in-person trainings, so we do it virtually. Everybody is supposed to take it, not just teachers, everybody: administrators, central office staff, lunchroom staff, security guards, literally everyone is required to take it. We've tried to make it really interactive, and I think we've been very successful at it. It was actually the highest-rated training on the PD platform. We have

activities—to sit and reflect, or follow these accounts
on social media, or go into your email now and update
your email signature to include your pronouns—that
make people do something in the moment.

If it's not possible to include all staff in PD, think about less
formal ways to share information with those who can't attend
the training: perhaps you could host a lunch-and-learn, distribute
flyers about respecting students' pronouns, have one-on-one conversations with colleagues, and so on.

Determining What to Teach

What do teachers do when we find that our class has varying
levels of comfort or knowledge about a topic? We differentiate.
Similarly, staff knowledge of this material, and their comfort
in discussing it, may vary significantly and require different
approaches based on existing comfort and knowledge. If you
have the time and resources, conducting a school climate survey,
inclusion audit, and/or self-assessments can be key to learning
your staff's existing knowledge about trans and non-binary
students, comfort in discussing gender identity, and any potential biases.

In general, an *audit* is a comprehensive examination of written
policies, informal practices, and actual experiences of community
members. Audits are usually conducted by an outside contractor
or consultant, and may include surveys or self-assessments as
part of the larger audit. A *survey* asks community members—
potentially including students, parents and families, teachers,
and other school staff—a series of questions and compiles the
results. Finally, a *self-assessment* allows an individual or small
group to reflect on their existing knowledge, community environments, and current practices. For more on selecting the right tool,
see the accompanying sidebar.

Audits, surveys, and self-assessments will help determine
the PD, policy changes, and learning needs of your specific
community, much like when teachers design instruction and

Choosing a School Climate Audit, Survey, or Self-Assessment

There are many options for school climate audits, surveys, and self-assessments as well as the possibility of customizing something tailored to your community. Here are some options for you to consider:

GLSEN's School Climate Survey hub, available at https://www.glsen .org/school-climate-survey, has results from the organization's National School Climate Survey as well as a free online Local School Climate Survey that can be used "to collect data on students' experiences in their local school communities." (Their much shorter GLSEN LGBTQ Inclusive School Assessments can be found in online version Bonus Resource 3 and at https://www.glsen.org/ activity/LGBTQ-inclusive-school-assessment.)

The CDC's LGBTQ Inclusivity in Schools self-assessment tool, available at https://www.cdc.gov/healthyyouth/disparities/mai/pdf/LGBTQ _Inclusivity-508.pdf, "was created to help school and district staff understand current policies, programs, and practices that may contribute to safe, inclusive environments where all youth can be successful." It includes an assessment for all staff as well as specific sections targeting administrators, educators, and school health services staff. (For a preview of the questions contained in this self-assessment, see online version Bonus Resource 2.)

intervention for students based on pre-assessment work. Doing a school climate survey or inclusion audit will allow school leaders to differentiate as well, and to choose a PD path for their staff based on staff and community needs.

Cheryl Greene, the director of Welcoming Schools, shared the following with us:

> We have a school climate assessment that we give
> schools before we do any work with them. We'll do a
> climate assessment before we work with them, we'll
> do it again midway, and we'll do it again at the end to
> be able to look at where folks have moved. It's a good
> snapshot of where folks are in terms of their comfort

level. It asks them specific questions like: You have
two parents come to your parent teacher conferences,
and one of the parents is trans. How do you feel about
that? The key to moving is them getting comfortable
responding to things or to addressing things.

I've been hearing that educators were having a
much easier time with binary trans kids [who identify
as either boys or girls], but that it's kids coming in
who are changing pronouns, are fluid, are using they/
them pronouns, are using both bathrooms depending
on where they feel that day, and educators just are like,
"How do I make this work?" And I think it just goes
back to the idea that people are who they say they are,
until they tell you otherwise. And I've kind of stuck
with that as my mantra.

Brittni Laura from A Queer Endeavor speaks to the bias angle
previously noted:

We're asking [the educators we work with], "What
biases and stereotypes do you bring to this work?
And are you viewing students in a deficit- or damage-
centered way? Or are you seeing what they bring
to the classroom as a positive, and with an equity
mindset?" That's hard, that personal work to look at
your own biases and judgments. The work starts there
and returns there and continues to dig again, in a
safe, low-stakes way. We talk about this soft space of
accountability, this balance of where we still have to be
accountable to our biases and to our actions and into
the harm that we create, but how do we do it in a way
that really centers tenderness and trying again, and
doing it better?

There is more information about both of these organizations
in Appendix 2.

The goal of an assessment or audit is not to rank your staff on
how much they already know, or to judge or punish those who
know less. Rather, it's to understand people's existing knowledge

and experience so we can successfully and effectively meet them where they are.

Note that, even if you don't have the budget to conduct a formal audit or survey, a self-assessment can still provide helpful framing and direction. You can also provide PD opportunities on the basics of gender identity and specific issues facing trans students. For more, see the issue of budget concerns in the "Addressing Real-World Challenges" section at the end of this chapter.

Incorporating the Voices of Trans Students

Trans Joy

The best thing about being trans is "teaching other people about it."

—Zephyr, 8.5

When educating school staff, it may feel difficult to center trans voices without forcing trans students to be responsible for training the adults in their community. On the one hand, both trans youth and adult advocates agree that student voices are central to changing the hearts and minds of educators, families, and communities. Hearing directly from students is often the most powerful part of any PD session, and can be key to understanding how abstract ideas play out in the classroom. As Jeff Perrotti (he/him), founding director of Massachusetts' Safe Schools Program for LGBTQ Students, shares:

> All the best practices, as well as the empathy and compassion that are engendered, are communicated best by people's stories, who are most affected by this. So that's at the core of all the professional development. And the work that I do is highlighting featuring the voices of trans young people and their family members.

On the other hand, we can't expect or rely on students to tell us everything they need and deserve. Some students may not know how to express their needs, while others may simply not feel comfortable as public advocates. In the following, Stella (she/her), a transgender teen and advocate for trans rights, describes how a teacher's well-intentioned request for help made her uncomfortable.

STELLA:

[We were getting ready for a sex ed lesson in science class] and my teacher was like, "Hey, Stella, would you look over the LGBTQ section of this? I want to make sure that I didn't get anything wrong or mess anything up."

What she really was asking was, "Hey, Stella, would you do the LGBTQ section for me so that I don't get it wrong?" And I was like, "Oh, I'm sorry. I'm your student and you're expecting me to make the curriculum for you. Got it."

Having my teacher essentially ask me to do the curriculum for her because she didn't want to get it wrong made me really upset because it's not my job, on two levels. One it isn't my job, because I'm your student. Secondly, it's not my job, because my life isn't educating everyone on being transgender.

STELLA'S MOTHER, LISA (SHE/HER):

At first you were excited, but there's a power dynamic. You really respected her, right? She was an important person to you, and she was trying to do her best. So at first we were okay because you wanted to please her, because you really respected her and cared about her. It was well intended, but it was also inappropriate. It was upsetting that the educator didn't recognize that.

It's critical that educators do our own learning, search out resources, attend PD, build our own toolbox, try new things, and adjust as we learn. While student voice is critical to this experience, it should be from students who have volunteered (and, ideally, received support and training) to be part of their educators' learning in a way that ensures student comfort and safety. For more on helping students who also want to be advocates, check out the box on student advocacy.

Fostering Student Advocacy

Trans students and their allies can and should have a voice in the policies and practices that impact their lives and their education. Here are some questions students can ask to help find the topic(s) they want to advocate on and the type of action(s) they want to take.

First, what do you care about?

This might be a specific issue, like ensuring everyone's names and pronouns are respected, or a broader topic, like how curricula are (or aren't) developed with trans identity in mind.

Second, what do you want to change?

Are there policies that need updating? Bad student experiences you want to avoid? Positive student experiences you want more people to be able to access? Is there not trans-inclusive sex ed? Has your city or state passed an anti-trans law that should be repealed? Do you want to advocate for students to get out and vote?

Third, find your audience.

How you approach advocacy within your family is different than with friends. Likewise, advocating with teachers may look different than speaking to the

(Continued)

(Continued)

school board or a PTA (parent-teacher alliance). Finally, speaking directly to elected officials may require a more formal approach or have different hoops to jump through.

Fourth, what kind of action do you want to take?

There's no right or wrong answer, as long as it aligns with what you want to change and the audience you want to reach. You can share your story in an op-ed, testimony, petition or sign-on letter. You can host a fundraiser to raise money for a specific cause or organization. You might start a letter-writing campaign or even host a giant rally.

Finally, decide what specifically you are asking for.

Once you've figured out the topic or issue you want to address, who you want to reach, and how you want to reach them, you need to come up with a focused ask to make. This could be concrete (vote "yes" on this bill or "no" on that one) or it could be more general (donate, vote, etc.).

Organizations, like the education advocacy nonprofit IDRA (Intercultural Development Research Association), also have great resources to support student advocacy, including IDRA's Six Steps to Promoting Student Activism:

1. Pinpoint Your Passion
2. Educate Yourself
3. Determine a Goal
4. Tap into Resources
5. Create an Action Plan
6. Take Action[1]

Determining Who Will Teach

If you hired an outside consultant to conduct an equity audit or school climate survey, they may also be able to provide training and PD on how to support trans students. But even if you didn't conduct an audit or survey (or you conducted one on your own), the good news is there are many local, statewide, and national organizations that provide a mix of free resources and paid training; some of those organizations are listed in the following, as are tips for finding other training options. (Suggestions on what to do if you can't hire an outside trainer are in the "Addressing Real-World Challenges" section at the end of the chapter.)

Regardless of the training options you consider, here are some questions to ask when making your decision as well as some things to think about related to each question:

Who is the facilitator and what is their connection to the trans community? Ideally, adult trans advocates are a key part of whatever training you select. That said, there are many amazing cis allies who provide excellent PD on supporting trans students; being trans is not a requirement to advocate for supporting trans students! What's critical is that the trainer or facilitator you work with has some existing relationship to the trans community, a history of advocating for trans rights, and an understanding of both the needs of trans students and how your school fits into the patchwork of local, state, and federal laws and policies.

How does the training include the voices of trans people, particularly trans youth and/or their families? Again, it is not critical that trans youth and/or their families participate in every training or PD opportunity. It is important, however, that voices of trans youth and their families inform the training you select, to ensure that the information is relevant to the specific needs of trans students in your community.

Does the training apply to the needs of your students? Make sure the trainer you select has specific knowledge on the needs of trans students. A trainer who is an expert on supporting adult trans employees in the workplace may not be familiar with classroom best practices, for example, sharing names and pronouns, how to intervene if you see a student being misgendered, and so on.

How does the training address intersectionality and apply to diverse student bodies? The trans community is as diverse as our society, meaning there are trans students of every age, race, ethnicity, religion, class, family structure, learning style, physical ability, and every other way of categorizing students. Any training on how to support trans students should speak to the needs of diverse student bodies.

What sample resources or documents does the training offer? Are there examples of relevant policies, for example, anti-bullying, student privacy, and so on? Does the trainer provide templates of gender support plans or other helpful resources?

How will the facilitator handle difficult questions, especially those that may push back against the idea of supporting trans students? Questions are important, even those that prompt uncomfortable conversation. A good trainer should be able to respectfully engage with difficult questions while staying firm on the need to support trans students.

What opportunities will there be to ask questions and receive follow-up support in the weeks or months following the training? We've all attended a lecture or PD session, only to realize days or weeks later that we have a question for the presenter. Is the trainer or facilitator you're working with able to offer any medium- or long-term support?

For a list of some PD provider options, see Appendix 2.

Trans Joy

I think a gem about being trans is the fearlessness of being fully yourself in all aspects of your identity, not just gender. I feel a great sense of pride in the impeccable and beautiful style, personality, and capacity for love that flourishes in the trans community.
—River (they/them)[1]

Challenges Facing School Staff

Most educators know that more and more is being expected of us, often with fewer and fewer resources. The data backs this up, with one 2020 report identifying that K–12 teachers "face new expectations and more demands from policymakers, parents, students, and schools, including addressing changes in curriculum standards, the emergence of more explicit teaching goals, and shifts in what it means to support all students in their development."[3] The COVID pandemic only made things worse, with many teachers also being asked to provide remote or hybrid instruction via video conferencing. As if that weren't enough, the steady pace of gun violence means teachers are often tasked to assist in active shooter drills.

In a perfect world, teachers and administrators would work together to balance this overwhelming list of tasks. Unfortunately, Dr. Harper Keenan of the University of British Columbia and the Trans Educator Network, has observed that this is not often the case:

> Teachers in the United States are not generally treated as intellectual professionals. They're often treated as kind of automatons to execute scripted curriculum. So a huge part of what [we've observed] was happening for educators was they felt incredibly micromanaged and controlled by their own administrations.

A lot of it is about the administration of schools in the US, because the teachers are feeling very disempowered, very controlled, and that carries down to their students.

That gets into the question of what is school for? What are we all doing here? Are we at school so that we can become citizens that align with a very narrow conception of particular identities and ways of being? Or are we here to learn how to be together as a society in public and develop the skills and content knowledge that we need in order to serve the public good?

Being micromanaged by administrators or overloaded with expectations from a state board of education may mean that not every educator or staff member may have the drive or capacity to proactively learn how and why to support trans students.

Meanwhile, some in your school community may never get onboard with supporting trans students and may even seek to disrupt trans students' education. In these cases, see Chapter 7: Disrupt.

Teaching While Trans

Though the issues and challenges facing trans teachers are similar, they're not exactly the same as those facing trans students. Dr. Keenan shared: "We see that in the trans workers study [the Trans Workers in Schools Project (TWISP), led equally by Dr. Keenan and his colleagues Dr. Mollie McQuillan and Dr. Mario Suarez] the ways that trans educators are kind of folding themselves into these boxes of normativity. And shaving off parts of who they are. Because they feel like they can't, it's either irrelevant, they need to just focus on the testing material, etc. Or there's this rigid understanding of who they are allowed to be at school."

Dr. Keenan highlighted the importance of considering trans rights as inherently connected to the labor rights movement. In a TENs survey, one of the highest factors that correlated with job satisfaction for trans teaches "was not things that we classically think about in affirming classrooms, things like getting your name right, getting your pronoun right, letting me use the right bathroom, letting me dress the way that I want to." Rather, it was union membership, "and that finding was four times more significant with trans workers of color. So trans workers of color had much higher levels of satisfaction correlated with their membership in a union."

Thoughts from a Trans Teacher in Texas

In early 2022, Texas Attorney General Ken Paxton arbitrarily (and in conflict with medical best practices) claimed that all gender-affirming care for trans youth was child abuse. This change would require Texas Child Protective Services to investigate families who are supportive of their trans children. As of September 2022 there was an injunction in place preventing these investigations from moving forward, but AG Paxton has appealed and the threat still looms large over many Texan families. Some Texan families with trans kids are so worried that they're leaving the state entirely.

We spoke with a transgender teacher who has taught in Texas for almost a decade. She teaches STEM courses to high school students and asked that her exact name and location be anonymized out of concern for her job and personal safety.

Tell us about your work

I teach at a public magnet school; anybody who lives in the district can apply to get in. Just a nerdy, really nerdy place. Currently, I'm teaching a ninth-grade engineering course. I picked up AP physics too this year, and that's all seniors.

How has your school been handling these issues?

I work at a really queer campus. I wasn't even the only trans teacher at one point. We have gender-neutral bathrooms now. And when the bathroom bills were going on, a few years ago, I went to my principal when it looked like it was

(*Continued*)

(*Continued*)

going to pass. I told her if this passes, I can't go on field trips, I can't do all this other stuff. And she was fairly supportive. She said, "I want you here. I think you're a great teacher. I think you're a great role model."

When it comes to supporting trans people, what do you wish existed? What do you think is missing?

A better understanding of the process of transition, and really just social transition. There doesn't need to be anything about any medical stuff in there. But just better understanding what that looks like and how long it takes. My experience with cis people is they tend to think that transition is, like, one day you're this, the next day you're that. That can cause people to misunderstand what students are doing with their presentation. So more first-person descriptions of what it is to be trans and in education, I think would be helpful.

What about things like going around and sharing pronouns or displaying "safe space" stickers?

Maybe I'm just old-school, but if I'm just welcoming, then students shouldn't feel uncomfortable sharing that [they're trans] with me, because I'm their teacher, right? If students are feeling uncomfortable sharing something with me on any topic like this, I'm doing something wrong. It doesn't have to be about gender identity—it could be about the family situation, or financial situation, whatever it is—but they should feel comfortable talking to me about that, just because I'm welcoming them into my classroom.

What does the future look like for you?

I am reluctantly considering leaving education, even though I don't want to. It is only because of the political pressures. Like, the stuff around reporting [students receiving gender-affirming care to child protective services]? And I know they [the Texas state legislature] are gonna try to pass a "Don't Say Gay" bill, they're going to try to pass another bathroom bill, they're going to try and put into statute the mandatory reporting. That combined with the rhetoric around grooming . . . I, as much as I love doing what I'm doing, and I love where I teach, I'm just like . . . I have too much to lose.

Putting It into Practice

Following are scenarios to consider about addressing real-world challenges and personal reflection questions to ask yourself. We encourage you to take some time to reflect and catch your breath before taking action.

Personal Reflection Questions

When educating school staff on how and why to support trans and non-binary students, it can be easy to forget that trans and non-binary students have more in common with their cisgender peers than not. Children's book author and former librarian Kyle Lukoff (he/him) talked about it this way:

> I see a lot of training on how to support trans kids presented as separate and discrete from how to support other kids, and I fully don't believe that that is true. If you already are the sort of teacher who knows how to make your classroom a welcoming space, and already knows how to listen to what children are telling you and reflect that back to them, you already know how to do that for your trans kids. And if you think you don't, that is just some reflection that you have to do.
>
> [Supporting trans students] is not necessarily a separate skill that you have to learn. I like to reassure educators: you already know how to do this, you just need to trust that you know how to do this. Don't let yourself be distracted by asking yourself, "What if I make a mistake?" Well, what if you make a mistake with any of your kids? You're gonna make a mistake and you are going to have to go from there.

To help you remember that you may have more skills and knowledge than you think, consider the following questions:

What biases and stereotypes do you bring to this work?

1. And are you viewing students in a deficit- or damage-centered way?

2. Or are you seeing what they bring to the classroom as a positive, and with an equity mindset?

3. How does supporting trans students align with your beliefs about students and education in general?

4. What experiences in your life inform what you already do or don't know about supporting trans students?

5. What is your comfort with talking about gender diversity? What about teaching it to your students?

6. What role do you play in the ecosystem of support for transgender students in your school community?

Addressing Real-World Challenges

When considering how to support trans students, educating the staff of a school community can be a great place to start. It can also be overwhelming, particularly when it doesn't seem like there is existing support or resources. Fortunately, you can almost always find ways to move forward, even in the most challenging of situations!

1. Let's say you have a limited—or nonexistent—PD budget for the year. How might you still provide resources or PD opportunities for staff that's focused on supporting transgender and non-binary students?

2. Let's say there are currently no *out* transgender students at your school—and someone says: "There's no need to address this topic now; we don't have any students like that." How might you respond to that? What allies could you find who can speak to the need for this type of training?

3. Given your current role and situation, what real-world challenges does this chapter bring up for you in your community? How might you approach those challenges? What resources currently exist from your school/district/board of education to handle these challenges?

4. If your current role changed, how might your thoughts on these challenges change? Think about how you might answer differently as a classroom teacher, a school principal, a district administrator, and so on.

Notes

1. Melivia Mujia, "Steps to promoting student activism—Infographic," IDCA (Intercultural Development Research Association), August 2019, https://www.idra.org/resource-center/steps-to-promoting-student-activism-infographic/; printable flyer at https://www.idra.org/wp-content/uploads/2019/10/10-Strategies-for-ICE-Raids.pdf. See also Melivia Mujia, "Steps for helping students become activists: A teen's advice," *IDRA Newsletter*, August 2019, https://www.idra.org/resource-center/steps-for-helping-students-become-activists/.

2. River, they/them, quoted in "Trans day of visibility: 7 trans people share what brings them joy" by Fortesa Latifi, *Teen Vogue*, March 31, 2022, https://www.teenvogue.com/story/transgender-day-of-visibility-joy.

3. "New report finds K–12 teachers face new expectations and more demands; training and workforce changes could help," News Release, National Academies of Sciences, February 2020, https://www.nationalacademies.org/news/2020/02/new-report-finds-k-12-teachers-face-new-expectations-and-more-demands-training-and-workforce-changes-could-help.

Affirm

"There are so many parts to trans youth, and being transgender isn't the only thing that makes us who we are. We are going to be able to thrive and, you know, produce the best math test score that we can and whatever it is, if we're supported and if we're accepted and affirmed. When we're not accepted and affirmed—especially in education settings controlled by the teacher, controlled by the school—it damages our ability to thrive and succeed. It's not only important in that everyone should be accepted and affirmed everywhere for who they are, it's also important because we want to do well in school, get a good education, and just be able to be kids in school."

—Sivan (he/him), trans youth

IN SOME ways, affirming transgender and non-binary students—that is, supporting and validating their gender and identity—is incredibly simple: Believe that your trans and non-binary students are who they say they are, and everything else flows from there. A therapist working with trans youth once told one of the authors, "People are who they say they are, until they tell you otherwise."

Hopefully, you are building and maintaining authentic relationships with all your students, so that they see you as a trusted adult who can listen and offer support; building those relationships with, and offering that support to, trans and non-binary students is not fundamentally any different. At the same time, the practical reality of creating both affirming policies and affirming practices for trans and non-binary students can be overwhelming.

99

This chapter digs into those practical realities, particularly as they relate to serving individual students.

FIGURE 5.1   Andy Passchier, There Is No One Way to be Non-Binary, 2021.[1]

For more information on the importance of affirming trans and non-binary students as their authentic selves, as well as general background information on the challenges transgender and non-binary students face, see the Introduction and Part I: Setting the Stage.

For information on broader topics such as school culture, curriculum, extracurricular activities, public communication, and more, see Chapter 6: Include.

Affirming Policies and Legislation

The Importance of Being Proactive

As educators and administrators, it can be tempting to wait until there's an out transgender or non-binary student at your school or in your district before you begin putting any trans-related policies into place. This should be avoided for a number of reasons. First, planning proactively—*before* there are any out trans or non-binary students—gives you the time and space to address concerns, engage with the community, and allow slow bureaucratic or administrative processes to play themselves out. More importantly, being proactive means that you will have the necessary policies in place as soon as you're made aware of a trans student; there won't have to be a significant delay between a student or family requesting support and the school or district being able to provide it. Finally, there may be trans students who are not out and who may only ever feel safe enough to come out if they know their school or district will have their back. Proactively putting policies into place not only ensures that you're better prepared to support trans students, it also sends an important message about your education community's commitment to those students.

Nikki Neuen (she/her), Executive Director at Trans Families and parent of a trans child, emphasized the importance of proactive policies, and the dangers of only taking stopgap measures as new issues arise:

> It is really common that families [with newly out trans children] will go into the schools, if the schools don't have adequate policies, and the school's response is, "Okay, your child can use the nurse's bathroom. Your child can be let out of class early to avoid bullying behavior." Any number of situations that your kid, alone, will be the only one, then, who will have these special circumstances that will accommodate them.
>
> Unfortunately, what that ends up doing is a stopgap; it only provides some immediate sense of relief. In the long term, though, that child—who may just want to be part of the rest of the group—becomes spotlighted over and over and over again. When we're talking about, "Oh, well, they can just use the teachers' bathroom that's over here by the office," that's a five-minute walk for those tiny legs from anywhere else in the school. That just makes them stand out even further. That's not a long-term solution, because it still creates this imbalance of, "Oh, here's the special unicorn, we're going to put a bubble around them, we're going to just push them through, push them through, and then we won't have to do this again."
>
> That's what that sort of stopgap measure does, over and over and over, is "We'll just get this one done. One and done out, we'll never think about it again."

More broadly, addressing the needs of trans and non-binary students often benefits the entire student body. Cory Grant (he/him) is the Dean of Students at Waring School in Massachusetts and noted:

> As I have worked to tackle seemingly trans specific problems like bathroom segregation, gendered dress code, segregated sports, unsupportive guardian

communication, and discriminatory school policy, I have come to realize that these issues have broader implications that go beyond the needs of trans and non-binary people. Everyone wants dignity, respect, care, and opportunity. Most solutions to problems that trans kids face tend to also improve the experience of everyone else. If we frame these problems as issues of mutual interest we can depoliticize and align efforts from a larger base of supporters. This is what I call the principle of overlapping interest. An example: When we improve our bathrooms by making them more accessible, comfortable, private, and safe, we all benefit as we also desegregate. In my experience there always exists an overlapping interest that when realized will lead us to a solution that benefits all.

Explicit versus Implicit Protections

When talking about school and district policies that protect trans students, as well as laws at the state and federal level, it's common to see distinctions between *explicit* protection, where a law or policy uses specific language to affirm the gender identity and gender expression of students, versus *implicit* protection, where a court or government agency has determined trans students are protected under existing language in laws or policies, even though the phrases gender identity or gender expression may never appear in the actual laws or policies.

For example, some states and school districts are passing laws and policies that *explicitly* forbid discrimination based on a student's gender identity or gender expression. A policy that explicitly includes trans people might read, "Our school community does not discriminate on the basis of race, color, religion, sex (including pregnancy, sexual orientation, or gender identity), gender expression, or national origin." Explicit protection is always the goal for advocates because it leaves less room for honest ignorance or intentional malice.

In another state, there may be general anti-discrimination laws or policies that don't *explicitly* include gender identity or gender expression, but a court ruling or state board of education guidance may say that the broad anti-discrimination language *implicitly* includes trans students. A policy that has been found to implicitly protect trans students might read, "Our school community protects all students from discrimination on the basis of who they are." Implicit protections may be all that is realistic in your community, given the makeup of a particular school board or state legislative body. Nevertheless, implicit protection leaves gaps where future court rulings or administrative decisions could roll back the rights of trans students, even if the laws or policies themselves don't change.

Model School and District Policies

When it comes to creating school or district policy to support trans students, there are a number of model policies and policy templates that you can use as a framework or a starting point for discussion. These model policies come from school districts and state boards of education, from nonprofits, from education associations,[2] and more.

This book uses the model policy put out by GLSEN and the National Center for Transgender Equality (NCTE) as a framework; this model policy provides good guidance without being overly long or complicated. That said, we encourage you to look at some of the different model policies that are available and determine what would be the best fit for your school or education community. Remember, no model policy will be perfect—for example, the GLSEN/NCTE model policy does not go into detail on what an inclusive curriculum might look like—but using a model policy means you won't have to start from scratch.

The sections of the GLSEN/NCTE model policy are listed here; the full text of the policy is available in online version Bonus Resource 1.[3]

A. Nondiscrimination Policies

B. Privacy and Confidentiality

C. Media and Public Communications

D. Names, Parent/Guardian Notification, School Records, and Pronouns

E. School Facilities (e.g., locker rooms, restrooms, etc.)

F. Physical Education, Sports, and Extracurricular Activities

G. Dress Code

H. Training and Professional Development

I. Notify and Engage K–12 Learning Communities on Policies to Support Transgender and Nonbinary Students

Nondiscrimination Policies

"First and foremost, we're here to educate children, so that everybody has an equal shot at excellence. We are here to equally celebrate and affirm all children and all families. And kids get the message about that in really subtle ways, how they are celebrated or how they are tolerated."

—Gabrielle Montevecchi (she/her), principal at Hannah Elementary in Beverly, MA, and parent of "two fantastic children, including one whom is a trans child"

Any nondiscrimination or anti-bullying policy should explicitly protect students (and, ideally, faculty, staff, and community members) from discrimination on the basis of sex, sexual orientation, gender identity, and gender expression. Those categories can be added to any existing nondiscrimination policy.

The GLSEN/NCTE model policy also notes that transgender students may have additional implicit protections under federal and/or state law; see elsewhere in this chapter for more information on explicit versus implicit protections, and for information on federal and state laws.

Bear in mind that laws impacting students may treat public schools and private schools differently. As Dr. Russ Toomey, Professor of Human Development and Family Science at the University of Arizona, explains, "As a baseline, we need nondiscrimination anti-bullying policies for all schools. It can't just be for publicly funded schools. It needs to be all schools."

Nondiscrimination policies can and should tie into any larger value statements that exist in your education community. Here's how Cheryl Greene, with Welcoming Schools, described that approach:

> [The language] we recommend for educators and administrators is, "In this school, we believe that all students should be treated with respect, valued, and authenticated for who they are." When there's push-back, we say, "It's our job as educators to ensure all of our students are in environments where they can thrive. People get to have their own personal beliefs and values, but in this school, here's what we believe." We work predominantly with public schools. So we can say that, as a public school, it's our job to ensure not just safety, but that these kids are in environments where they can flourish. How can we help support your student?

Privacy and Confidentiality

Some trans students are out to *everyone* in their school community. Some trans students are not out to *anyone* in their school community. Many trans students are somewhere in between, with a select group of friends and adults "in the know." There is no correct or proper level of out-ness, as long as decisions are made thoughtfully and with the involvement of the student in question.

When considering privacy policies as they relate to trans students, it can be helpful to ask who in a school community *needs* to know that a student is trans, versus who might be curious or simply *want* to know. For example, a school nurse might need to access health information that includes whether or not a student is trans. On the other hand, a math teacher probably doesn't need to know that a student is trans, particularly if the attendance sheet only includes the student's preferred name.

Meanwhile, some students may want to keep information about their identity private *from* parents or guardians. See the following section on Names, Parent/Guardian Notification, School Records, and Pronouns for more on navigating how to support a student who isn't out to their parents or guardians, or doesn't trust their parents or guardians with that information.

Trans Joy

My dog makes me really happy. It was just his birthday and I got him a new bed, a new hoodie, a new collar, and an ice cream cone from Dairy Queen.

—Elliot (he/him), 18[4]

Media and Public Communications

School policies should clearly outline who is authorized to speak on behalf of the school for both internal and external communications. To best support trans and non-binary students, the policy should explicitly emphasize student privacy and that personal information about any student (trans or cis) should never be shared publicly.

Names, Parent/Guardian Notification, School Records, and Pronouns

Students should be able to change their name and pronoun in school records, attendance sheets, and other school documents without going through a legal name change. Students should be able to use their preferred name and pronouns in any school situation, and on any school documents or paperwork, except where a legal name is explicitly required by law.

Tamara Jazwinski (she/her), a school counselor in a suburb of Chicago, noted that, "Our district has become very flexible and positive in terms of if a student wants to change their name: they can change it, no question. The student doesn't have to have all the legal paperwork to make these changes, and gender markers have also been removed from all transcripts. Students can change their IDs, their emails, their online accounts, which is phenomenal. It's huge that kids can do this without parent permission."

That said, parents and guardians generally have a legal right to access student records, and schools may be hesitant to allow students to change names or pronouns without parental permission.[5] Even if school policy or state law requires parental permission or notification, however, school policies can still require that students are notified before personal information is shared with parents or guardians. Likewise, school staff can and should speak with trans students about the support they do or don't receive at home to better understand the consequences of potentially outing a student to their parents or guardians.

Rae Jones (they/them), a classroom teacher for more than a decade, explains what this can be like for adult allies of trans students, sharing, "I may be talking to a 15 year old and have to ask, 'So do you want to potentially out yourself to your unsafe family, in order to be affirmed by your classmates and your teachers, or not?' That's a horrible conversation to have, and I have that conversation a lot right now. One of my students said, 'Yeah, I don't really want to talk to my mom [about being trans] but if she finds out through this [me changing my name in the school system], that's okay.' We'll talk about using a name change to come out. But asking 15 year olds to have that clarity is really unfair."

Unfortunately, with the current political climate, some teachers may be faced with a difficult choice to either respect a student's name, pronouns, and privacy, but break a law requiring parental notification, or follow the law and notify a parent or guardian, but put the student at risk for mistreatment by those family members. While there have always been students who ask to be called something other than their legal name, the COVID pandemic—and remote learning specifically—only accelerated this trend, as Dr. Russ Toomey, Professor of Human Development and Family Science at the University of Arizona, explains:

> COVID amplified the issue because there was the emergence of everybody being home; if a child was maybe going by one name and pronouns at school, but not at home, then you have a conflict when school takes place at home. There is a potential lack of safety, of violence happening in the home, because of that disconnect.

But being able to change a name and pronouns in a school system can make the difference between student participation and non-involvement, as noted by the trans teacher we spoke to in Texas:

> I had a student who came up to me at the beginning of the school year after an assignment with an online discussion component. The student asked, "Are we gonna have a lot of these throughout the year?"
>
> And I said, "Yeah, every so often."
>
> And he said, "Well, I can't change my name [on the online discussion platform], unless we do a legal name change." So every time he would add to the discussion, he'd see a name that was not his and it would be non-affirming. His concern was not so much about him seeing that name as much as it was about other students seeing it and calling him by it. That limits his ability to engage as a student. Even though like, you know, our campus is super queer-friendly, this issue was still there. It's still part of the pinpricks that add up.

Finally, even if your school or district wants to be as supportive as possible, changing school or district systems to allow this can be a long, difficult process. Booker Marshall, with Chicago Public Schools (CPS), shared the slow-and-steady progress CPS was able to make when switching to a new information management system:

> A lot of the issues we were having early on, like late 2017 and '18, were around our student information system not being great. It did the thing of having the legal name with "preferred name" in parentheses next to it. So it's outing every trans student that doesn't have a legal name change.
>
> We had an opportunity when CPS decided to switch to Aspen [a school information management system], and they were building out Aspen to accommodate trans students. So it was built out that way. We ended up making an Affirmed Name field in Aspen. Students that don't have a legal name change or gender marker change can change that in the system. It took four years to update all the systems [in the school district].
>
> What that means, though, is that there are places where—when you choose to use the Affirmed Name in Aspen—it will show up on things that parents can see. So students who have privacy concerns with their family members are not served well by this. It was too complicated, too complex, to devise these IT systems that are separate from each other in a way that actually protects student privacy, but at the end of the day (because of FERPA [Family Educational Rights and Privacy Act]) anything that's on a student record, officially, is legally accessible to parents and guardians.
>
> But for those who do have supportive family members, or who don't have safety concerns with family, they are able to have their name everywhere; it shows up on their report cards and progress reports, everywhere legally permissible. Even transcripts have both the legal and affirmed name. I've had an incredible experience working with our IT professionals here. I feel very fortunate to have them.

School Facilities (e.g., locker rooms, restrooms, etc.)

In a perfect world, a school facilities policy for trans students would likely be quite short:

1. Everyone has access to the facilities that correspond with their gender identity and in which they feel most comfortable, and

2. Anyone can access private facilities on request.

Item #1 ensures that transgender and non-binary students can access the appropriate facilities, while item #2 offers privacy to any student, for whatever reason, and whether or not the student is trans. This type of policy means that trans students won't be required to use different facilities (e.g., a nurse's office bathroom or a coach's changing room), but means that students who are uncomfortable in public facilities can have privacy, whether their discomfort is due to their gender identity, their religion, their body type, or simply their personal preference.

Gabrielle Montevecchi, the principal at Hannah Elementary in Beverly, MA, noted that some schools make access to bathrooms or other facilities more complicated than it needs to be:

> We talk about using language that is completely gender inclusive. It's so simple to do, but it takes a little bit of scripting. So many things are just so binary that do not have to be. I talk with principals about this all the time; they ask, "What do you do about the bathroom thing?"
>
> And the simple script we use at the school is, "People use the bathroom that they feel comfortable going in." And that is the end of it. Just very simple language to use with staff, to use with students, and to make sure that parents hear you say that as well. And then I'm the person who has the conversation, if anyone has a concern about that.

Principal Montevecchi also offers herself as an ally in this process, ensuring that any students, staff, or community with questions or concerns can come directly to her, rather than confronting a trans student or assuming all school staff will be comfortable explaining who should use which bathroom.

Physical Education, Sports, and Extracurricular Activities

Like the preceding "School Facilities" section, in a perfect world the physical education, sports, and extracurricular activities policy would be quite short:

1. Students participate in all school programs and activities—including physical education, sports, and extracurricular activities—according to their gender identity.

2. No legal changes, medical treatment, or specific documentation shall be required for participation or to "prove" a student's gender identity.

Unfortunately, we do not live in a perfect world; see Chapter 7: Disrupt for more on how anti-trans legislation is targeting trans and non-binary students. The important thing is to stress that trans and non-binary students should never be excluded from participating in a school program, event, field trip, overnight trip, or any other activity simply because of who they are.

For participation in school sports, many schools follow the policies set by the state athletic association. These policies can be found online and may differ widely from state to state. Regardless of the state policies, however, individual schools (and even individual teachers or school staff) should make it clear that they fully support trans and non-binary participation in student athletics, even if the state legislature or state athletic association does not. For more on responding to anti-trans laws and policies, see Chapter 7: Disrupt.

Dress Code

School dress codes should be gender neutral and enforced equally among all students. A comprehensive dress code policy is also an opportunity to support all students, not just those who are trans or non-binary. For example, dress codes are sometimes used to body-shame or otherwise police the bodies of female students.[6]

On the other hand, some schools are using their dress codes as an opportunity to explicitly ban body-shaming and better support marginalized students—in 2017, Evanston Township High School, in Evanston, Illinois, (coauthor Rebecca Kling's home town!) revised its dress code to, among other things, say that it should be enforced "in a manner that does not reinforce or increase marginalization or oppression of any group based on race, sex, gender identity, gender expression, sexual orientation, ethnicity, religion, cultural observance, household income or body type/size."[7]

Training and Professional Development

To ensure that schools provide adequate training and professional development, school policy should include the frequency and broad content to be covered in professional development on supporting trans and non-binary students. Ideally, training should take place annually and the information should include terms and definitions, appropriate language to use, curriculum information and resources, guidance for speaking with parents and community members, and discussion and processing space for staff.

Local, State, and Federal Law

This section provides an overview of the legal landscape trans students may face in the United States. Laws and policies are complicated (to say the least!) and this book does not offer legal advice. Likewise, the legal landscape is changing fast and this section may already be outdated by the time you read it. We encourage you to do your own research (see later section for tips on how) and speak to a lawyer for any specific legal advice.

Federal Law

In the United States, there is no federal law that *explicitly* protects trans students. Nevertheless, federal protections for trans students still exist. In particular, courts have consistently found that

Title IX—which prohibits sex discrimination in most schools—
also prohibits anti-trans discrimination because treating someone
differently due to their gender identity or expression is ultimately
a type of sex discrimination. The U.S. Department of Education
has issued guidance along those lines as well, saying that Title IX
prohibits "1) discrimination based on sexual orientation; and (2)
discrimination based on gender identity."[8]

As a long-term federal goal, a bill called the Equality Act
would explicitly prohibit discrimination on the basis of sex,
sexual orientation, and gender identity in education as well as
employment, housing, jury service, and more. Until the Equality
Act passes, however, Title IX remains a key legal tool in supporting trans students.

In the United States, the Family Educational Rights and
Privacy Act (FERPA) is also an important tool for supporting
trans students. FERPA, a federal law that protects the privacy
of a student's educational records, was written and enacted in
the 1970s and doesn't specifically address the needs of trans students.[9] Still, FERPA can be useful to parents or guardians who are
supportive of a trans child.

For example, FERPA says schools can share student records
with "school officials with legitimate educational interest."
This means that a student's trans identity should not be shared
with every school employee, as that does not serve a legitimate
educational interest.

Lizette Trujillo (she/her), a parent of a trans child and
member of HRC Foundation's Parents for Transgender Equality
National Council, explained that "FERPA is your golden ticket
to privacy, because if a parent comes to the front desk and says,
'I hear there's a trans kid in my child's class,' the school cannot
give out that personal information [about someone else's child].
Now, I feel very strongly that Daniel [my trans child] should have
the agency to disclose to whomever he wants and not feel shame
about his identity, so we have lots of talks about what agency and
disclosure look like. But those talks about privacy that we had
with the school were necessary and helpful."

Individualized Education Programs (IEPs) and 504 plans stem from laws ensuring that students requiring modified instruction or curriculum (generally covered under an IEP) or other accommodations (generally covered under 504 plans) are able to do so. While neither IEPs nor 504 plans were established with the goal of supporting trans students, both may be useful advocacy tools in supporting trans students.

State and Local Laws and Policies

In addition to federal laws, policies, and guidelines, there is an often-confusing mix of school, district, and city policies and guidelines that exist about trans students, meaning that supporting trans students may look very different depending on where in the country (or even where in a particular state) you're located.

School or Community Laws and Policies

Before you begin publicly advocating on behalf of trans students, it can be helpful to know the legal landscape you're facing in your community. At the state level, maps from the Movement Advancement Project (MAP) are a great place to begin your research; they can be found at https://www.lgbtmap.org/equality-maps (see Figure 5.2).

The available national maps link to individual state profiles (as well as profiles for DC, Puerto Rico, and other U.S. territories) with information about laws and policies impacting LGBTQ+ people, including a section focusing on laws impacting youth, for example, non-discrimination, anti-bullying laws, curriculum standards, "Don't Say Gay" bills, trans athletics bans, and more. You may also find useful information by conducting an Internet search on "transgender students in <STATE>" or "<STATE> laws on transgender students" as well as searching for the specific language of anti-bullying or anti-discrimination laws and policies.

At the district or school level, you can search for local anti-discrimination or anti-bullying policies, as well as for "<SCHOOL DISTRICT> transgender policy" or "<SCHOOL DISTRICT> transgender support plan."

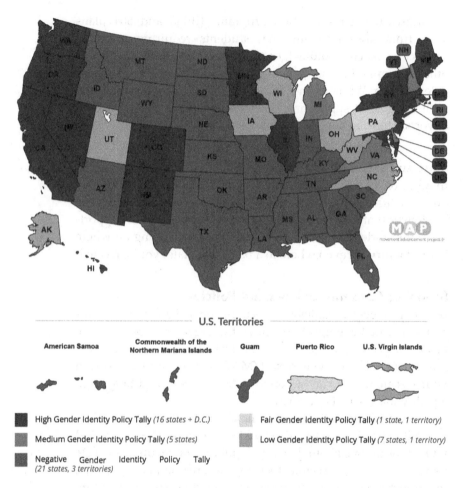

FIGURE 5.2 Movement Advancement Project (MAP) generated on May 26, 2023.

Over the past few years, there has also been a catastrophic rise in legislative and policy attacks on LGBTQ people in the United States: in 2018, fewer than 20 anti-LGBTQ bills were introduced in state legislatures across the country. In 2022, 174 anti-LGBTQ bills were introduced. By the middle of May 2023, organizations such as the ACLU and Trans Legislation Tracker identified more than 500 anti-LGBTQ bills introduced in 49 states.[10] Many of these bills specifically targeted trans students. For more on anti-trans policies and laws and how to respond to them, see Chapter 7: Disrupt.

Hopefully, when you research your area, you'll find that your state and local communities are already creating laws and policies that explicitly protect trans students. At the very least, you'll have a better sense of what opportunities you have and what obstacles you may face.

Affirming Practices

"Policies are only as good as their implementation. There's a lot of work that needs to be done in order for policies to land safely. We [A Queer Endeavor] worked with a K–8 school a couple of years ago that was really forward thinking and wanted to have all-gender restrooms. But they realized that they didn't have any education around, like, what are these bathrooms? Why do they matter? There was a gap between policy and practice. Often the people who make the policies are completely removed from the people who are actually putting them into practice."

—Sara Staley (she/her), cofounder and
co-director of A Queer Endeavor

Once your policies are in place, how do you ensure they're actually implemented and followed? Likewise, how do you adjust as needed, once an abstract policy is applied to students and schools? This is where the rubber meets the road.

First and foremost, it's important to keep lines of communication open and allow for student input. When working to support trans students (or cis students, or any students) it can be tempting to believe that, simply because we aren't hearing about a problem, the problem must not exist. Students can become skilled in hiding stress or negative experiences, so maintaining authentic relationships between students and faculty is the most effective way of understanding what is truly going on at a school. Ongoing formal opportunities for student input—such as school climate surveys or soliciting regular feedback—can also help staff and educators determine what may still need to be addressed.

It's also important to ensure that policies—and school staff—are flexible enough to adjust as needed. We spoke with Sivan (he/him), a trans student, about his experience working with a school administration that hadn't worked with a trans student before, and whose expectations didn't always match his own:

> I decided that I was going to be stealth [going into high school], and I didn't want anyone at school to know. But we also realized that we should talk to the administration to just make sure everything is smooth. That was a little bit tough, because I would have rather just gone into the school that had experience [with trans students]. But because it didn't, we did talk to the Dean of Students. The school had, and has, really great intentions, but it was a lot to educate them about.
>
> I remember, for example, we were talking in that first meeting, and she [the Dean of Students] was like, "Yeah, we have the gender-neutral bathroom in the basement."
>
> And I was, like, "I know there's no ill intent behind this, but I'm actually a boy. So I'd like to use the boys' bathroom. Because you're saying every time I'd use the bathroom, I'd go down to the basement?"
>
> And then once she understood that, she was like, "Oh, of course, like, you can use the boys' bathroom." So it was a lot of education. That was really important. And also, at the same time, a little bit hard to do.

Gabrielle Montevecchi, the principal at Hannah Elementary in Beverly, MA, observed similar problems around restroom access, and the importance of making sure policies work in the real world:

> My experience was with a high school student who used the only non-gendered bathroom and had to go up to the second floor, five minutes away, missing important time on an AP test. This kind of thing still goes on—conversations around where and why and who gets to use it [the non-gendered bathroom], and why it gets closed because kids are using that bathroom to vape or whatever—but that's unacceptable.

> Children simply go where they need to go. They
> respectfully go where they need to go. And I have not
> encountered difficulties at my school about that.

We also heard that teaching staff how and why policies are being put into place can be just as important as the policies themselves, such as with Alisa Kotler-Berkowitz (she/her), the parent of a trans child:

> When we talk about teachers and we talk about pol-
> icies they have to follow, teachers are constantly given
> more things to do; things are thrown at them all the
> time. But instead of just getting training about what
> the policy is, [my child's teachers] actually had a few
> days of intensive, integrative, education to really
> understand. It can be as simple as people just sharing
> their stories. Because once you meet a person it's
> much easier to then implement a policy, right? It's
> not this random thing, and you just understand it
> more. So I think that piece of true understanding is
> often missing.

Finally, Sara Staley (she/her) with A Queer Endeavor reminded us that simply having policies on the books is not enough if community members and staff aren't aware of them:

> This one district [we worked with] actually has a really
> progressive policy around supporting trans and gender
> non-conforming youth. They've had it on the books
> since 2012. But not a lot of people knew about it and
> they didn't have a systemic plan for implementation for
> that policy. People who did know about the policy were
> parents of queer and trans youth, and they were coming
> to the district because it was a safe and supportive place.
>
>   The district reached out to us when we launched
> A Queer Endeavor, so we were able to build a
> university/district partnership with them around
> implementing that policy. There was such a need
> in the community for support and education and
> teacher learning.

Once affirming policies are put into place, a school or district may need follow-up surveys and data-gathering to ensure that the policies are actually accomplishing what they set out to do.

Gender Support Plans

One way to help ensure that gender-affirming policies are being carried out in practice is by working with a trans or non-binary student to craft a gender support plan, a document outlining a student's understanding of their own gender and identity, the student's family support (or lack thereof), how public or private information about the student's gender will be, and more. There are a number of free gender support plan templates available, and they may be customized to the needs of a specific student or school. Broadly speaking, a gender support plan requires school staff to consider all aspects of a transgender or non-binary student's experiences both in and outside of school, and how the school can support and affirm that student. See the online version Bonus Resource 4 for an example gender support plan.

While no one policy or procedure will guarantee a trans or non-binary student receives the support they need, a gender support plan is an important tool in the toolbox, as Tamara Jazwinski, a school counselor in a suburb of Chicago, explains:

> When we first started to do gender support plans, there would be one or two active plans in place per school year. We now have an average of about 12 gender support plans in place every year, which is absolutely outstanding.
>
> Students often ask me to tell them about the gender support plan, simply wanting to know what they mean? What do they do?
>
> We start by having a conversation about the ins and outs of the plan and I tell the student, "Even if you just want to start by getting your ID changed to your affirmed name, we can do that easily." This action in and of itself can be quite calming for many students since they use their IDs daily.

Four Schools, Four Experiences

Let's look at four real school districts to imagine what legal support or opposition trans and non-binary students, and their allies and advocates, might find there. This section is intended to help you think about what policies and laws exist in your community, and what support or opposition you can expect when working to support trans and non-binary students.

Chicago Public Schools (CPS)—Chicago, Illinois

Both CPS and the State of Illinois have established explicit laws, policies, and guidelines that support and affirm transgender students in K–12 institutions. For example, the Illinois State Board of Education's 2020 guidelines note that both the Illinois Human Rights Act and Illinois anti-bullying laws protect students from discrimination on the basis of gender identity, gender expression, and sexual orientation. CPS offers a Supporting Gender Diversity Toolkit and, in 2019, Illinois passed a law requiring Illinois schools to teach students about LGBTQ+ history by the time they finish 8th grade.[11] CPS also has a gender support plan template available for trans students. While none of these laws, policies, or resources *guarantee* that every trans student will receive the support at school that they deserve, strong policies at the local, city, and state levels ensure that adults advocating for and with trans youth will have a firm legal foundation for their advocacy.

Booker Marshall, LGBTQ+ & Sexual Health Program Manager with CPS, noted that programming and resources aimed at supporting trans students in CPS has grown significantly in recent years due to increased demand.

Dayton Public Schools—Dayton, Ohio

Neither Dayton Public Schools, nor the State of Ohio, have any explicit protections for trans students. While Ohio school districts are required to establish anti-bullying policies, Ohio has not explicitly listed gender identity or expression (or, indeed, any specific categories) as protected from bullying or discrimination, nor does the Dayton Public Schools anti-bullying policy. While these anti-bullying policies, and Title IX at the federal level, may be useful in advocating on behalf of trans students, the lack of explicit protections may make advocacy more difficult than in locations where explicit protections exist. The City of Dayton's anti-discrimination ordinances—which do protect from discrimination in "public accommodations" on the basis of "sexual orientation [and] gender identity"—may also be useful when advocating on behalf of trans students.[12]

Unfortunately, in December 2022, the Ohio State Board of Education passed a nonbinding resolution supporting any bills from the Ohio State Legislature that would ban trans youth from participating in student athletics.[13]

All this means that trans students in Dayton have a mix of implicit and explicit protections, as well as at least one explicitly anti-trans vote from the State Board of Education, which may make legal advocacy more difficult than in places with stronger explicit protections.

Duval County Public Schools—Jacksonville, Florida

When it comes to supporting trans students, the State of Florida has some of the worst laws in the country. The state's "Don't Say Gay" bill restricts the ability of teachers to talk about LGBTQ identity and opens schools up to civil suits from anti-LGBTQ community members. The Florida State Board of Education now requires schools to notify parents if trans students are using bathrooms or locker rooms that are "not separated by biological sex at birth." The Florida Legislature passed an anti-trans bathroom bill that applies to "restrooms and changing facilities in state and local government buildings, schools, colleges, and detention centers." And in 2022, the Duval County School Board—which serves the approximately 125,000 students in Jacksonville, Florida—unanimously passed a policy requiring schools to notify parents of trans students if those students want to use a different name or pronoun.[14]

These laws and policies mean that—even with supportive teachers or school administrators—it will be particularly difficult to support trans students in a Duval County Public School. Nevertheless, it is always possible to treat trans students with respect and to ensure they know that, even when the laws aren't supportive, you as an adult in that student's life are still on their side. Local community organizations, including the local LGBTQ community center and other advocacy groups, may be able to provide additional support or resources.

TJ Johnson of the YES! Institute, which is based in Florida, has spoken with educators impacted by these laws, saying they "fear not knowing what the right thing to do is and being afraid of losing their jobs if they do the wrong thing."

Austin Integrated School District (ISD)—Austin, Texas

A trans or non-binary student in Austin, Texas, will likely face a mix of support and opposition. As of February 28, 2023, Texas does not have any explicitly anti-trans curricular laws (the type of "Don't Say Gay" bill that exists in Florida), but similar laws have been proposed in the statehouse. Unfortunately, Texas does have a law barring trans student athletes from participating in sports that align with their gender identity. And while Texas does not currently have any anti-trans restroom laws, it also does not have any explicit protections for trans or non-binary students, or requirements that they be supported in school. In addition, Texas Attorney General Ken Paxton issued guidance in early 2022 falsely claiming that providing trans youth gender-affirming care is child abuse, opening the door to investigations by Texas Department of Family and Protective Services and the possibility that trans youth might be forcibly removed from supportive homes. (This issue is still playing out in court.) As of February 28, 2023, six bills that would harm trans students have been introduced by the Texas legislature, although it's not clear if they will be signed into law.[15]

That said, Austin ISD does have an Office of Equality, established in 2019, that aims to "achieve racial and social equity" regardless of a student's "sexual orientation, sex, gender identity & expression," among other characteristics. [16]

All of this means that an educator in Austin ISD looking to support trans and non-binary students may have some administrative backing from the Office of Equity but the student will not have explicit legal protection and, depending on how things play out in the state legislature, may face legislative opposition to their right to a quality education.

Putting It into Practice

Following are scenarios to consider about addressing real-world challenges and personal reflection questions to ask yourself. We encourage you to take some time to reflect and catch your breath before taking action.

Personal Reflection Questions

1. What gaps in your understanding of your school, district, and state laws exist for you?

2. What are you going to do to close those gaps?

3. How does where you live impact how you feel you can approach affirming trans youth? Explain.

4. This chapter discusses policy versus practice. Where do you find evidence of these differences in your setting around trans and non-binary youth?

Addressing Real-World Challenges

1. You've found that the laws in your state *explicitly* deny rights to trans and non-binary students, or are trying to remove rights. What can you do given your role? (For ideas, see Chapter 7: Disrupt.)

2. You are involved in opening a new school and crafting a mission statement. Write that mission statement, including what you've learned in this chapter as support.

3. For privacy reasons, a transgender student in your school, Z, has decided to use the nurse's bathroom. Z doesn't want other people to know that they are trans. Another student asks why Z is using the nurse's bathroom. How do you respond?

4. You have a transgender student and unclear policies regarding bathrooms and locker rooms. The lockdown drills at your school note that bathrooms and locker rooms are places to hide. During a lockdown drill, the transgender student wasn't allowed into either locker room and was left outside. What can be changed or what policy could be put into place to ensure this student's safety and prevent this dangerous situation?[17]

5. Given your current role and situation, what real-world challenges does this section bring up for you in your community? How might you approach those challenges? What resources currently exist from your school/district/board of education to handle these challenges?

6. If your current role changed, how might your thoughts on these challenges change? Think about how you might answer differently as a classroom teacher, a school principal, a district administrator, and so on.

Notes

1. Andy Passchier, There Is No One Way to be Non-Binary, Instagram, https://www.instagram.com/p/CurmNZ8LJoh/?hl=en.

2. "Supporting transgender, nonbinary and gender nonconforming students," Illinois State Board of Education, n.d., https://www.isbe.net/supportallstudents; "LGBTQIA resources for team members," The Commons, Denver Public Schools, n.d., http://thecommons.dpsk12.org/site/default.aspx?pageid=2017; Empire Justice Center, the Empire State Pride Agenda, and the NYCLU, "Model policy for creating a safe and supportive school environment for transgender and gender nonconforming students," n.d., https://www.nyclu

.org/sites/default/files/dignityforall_modelpolicy.pdf; National Education Association, "Legal guidance on transgender students' rights," April 2018, https://www.nea.org/resource-library/legal-guidance-transgender-students-rights.

3. "Model Local Education Agency Policy on Transgender and Nonbinary Students," GLSEN, Revised October 2020, https://www.glsen.org/activity/model-local-education-agency-policy-on-transgender-nonbinary-students.

4. Eliot (he/him), 18, quoted in "Trans day of visibility: 7 trans people share what brings them joy" by Fortesa Latifi, *Teen Vogue*, March 31, 2022, https://www.teenvogue.com/story/transgender-day-of-visibility-joy.

5. Katie J. M. Baker, "When students change gender identity, and parents don't know," *New York Times*, January 22, 2023, https://www.nytimes.com/2023/01/22/us/gender-identity-students-parents.html.

6. Sasha Jones, "Do school dress codes discriminate against girls?" *Education Week*, August 31, 2018, https://www.edweek.org/leadership/do-school-dress-codes-discriminate-against-girls/2018/08.

7. Jake Holland, "ETHS opts for new, more progressive dress code," *The Daily Northwestern*, September 17, 2017, https://dailynorthwestern.com/2017/09/17/city/eths-opts-new-progressive-dress-code/.

8. "Know your rights: Schools," National Center for Transgender Equality, n.d., https://transequality.org/know-your-rights/schools; "U.S. Department of Education Confirms Title IX Protects Students from Discrimination Based on Sexual Orientation and Gender Identity," US Department of Education, June 16, 2021, https://www.ed.gov/news/press-releases/us-department-education-confirms-title-ix-protects-students-discrimination-based-sexual-orientation-and-gender-identity.

9. "Family Educational Rights and Privacy Act (FERPA)," U.S. Department of Education, last modified August 25, 2021, https://www2.ed.gov/policy/gen/guid/fpco/ferpa/index.html.

10. Anne Branigin and N. Kirkpatrick, "Anti-trans laws are on the rise. Here's a look at where—and what kind," *Washington Post*, October 14, 2022, https://www.washingtonpost.com/lifestyle/2022/10/14/anti-trans-bills/; "Mapping Attacks on LGBTQ Rights in U.S. State Legislatures," ACLU, last updated May 19, 2023, https://www.aclu.org/legislative-attacks-on-lgbtq-rights; "2022 anti-trans legislation," Trans Legislation Tracker, n.d., https://trans legislation.com/bills/2022; "2023 anti-trans bills tracker," Trans Legislation Tracker, https://translegislation.com/.

11. "Supporting transgender, nonbinary and gender nonconforming students," Illinois State Board of Education, March 1, 2020, https://www.isbe.net/Documents/ISBE-Guidance-Supporting-Transgender-Nonbinary-Gender-Nonconforming-Students.pdf; "Supporting Gender Diversity Toolkit," Office of Student Health and Wellness, Chicago Public Schools, https://www.cps.edu/globalassets/cps-pages/services-and-supports/health-and-wellness/healthy-cps/healthy-environment/lgbtq-supportive-environments/supportinggenderdiversitytoolkit2.pdf; Hannah Leone, "New law requires Illinois schools teach contributions of gay, transgender people: 'It is past time children know the names of LGBTQ+ pioneers,'" *Chicago Tribune*, September 3, 2019, https://www.chicagotribune.com/news/breaking/ct-lgbtq-history-illinois-schools-law-20190826-m2k4qtpiifhkzp5a76dwtwlbwy-story.html.

12. "Section 3313.666 | District policy prohibiting harassment, intimidation, or bullying required," Ohio Revised Code, Title 33 Education-Libraries, Chapter 3313 Boards of Education, Ohio Laws & Administrative Rules, November 4, 2012, https://codes.ohio.gov/ohio-revised-code/section-3313.666; "JFCF-R hazing and bullying (Harassment, Intimidation and Dating Violence)," Dayton Public Schools, last reviewed March 10, 2020, posted February 1, 2022; https://www.dps.k12.oh.us/wp-content/uploads/2022/02/BoardDocs%C2%AE-Policy_-JFCF-R-Hazing-And-Bu . . . pdf; "Civil rights enforcement," City of Dayton Human Relations Council, n.d., https://daytonhrc.org/civil-rights-enforcement/.

13. Jo Ingles, "Ohio education board passes controversial resolution against federal anti-discrimination policy, The Statehouse News Bureau, December 13, 2022, https://www.statenews.org/government-politics/2022-12-13/ohio-education-board-passes-controversial-resolution-against-federal-anti-discrimination-policy.

14. "Florida's equality profile," MAP (Movement Advancement Project), n.d., https://www.lgbtmap.org/equality_maps/profile_state/FL; "What you need to know about Florida's 'Don't Say Gay' Law," National Education Association, updated June 2022, https://www.nea.org/sites/default/files/2022-06/FL%20Dont%20Say%20Gay%20KYR%20-%20Updated2022.06.pdf; Leo Santos, "Florida education board approves rule changes for 'parental rights' amid LGBTQ criticism," WTSP, updated October 19, 2022, https://www.wtsp.com/article/news/education/florida-department-education-rule-changes-parental-rights/67-89a31b37-70ab-46fd-a9b9-7e2f44e33f78; Andrew Atterbury, "Florida Republicans pass bill targeting transgender bathroom use," *Politico*, May 3, 2023, https://www.politico.com/news/2023/05/03/florida-gop-transgender-bathroom-bill-00095168; Joe McLean, "Duval School Board OKs new policy to line up with controversial state law critics say could harm LGBTQ+ students," News 4JAX, updated July 12, 2022, https://www.news4jax.com/news/local/2022/07/12/duval-school-board-votes-in-favor-of-student-support-service-policy/.

15. Alex Nguyen and William Melhado, "Two Texas bills would restrict lessons about sexual orientation and gender identity in public schools," *Texas Tribune*, January 9, 2023, https://www.texastribune.org/2023/01/09/texas-bills-sexual-orientation-gender-identity-florida-law/; Allyson Waller, "Trans kids and supporters say new Texas law will keep them out of school sports," *Texas Tribune*, January 18, 2022, https://www.texastribune.org/2022/01/18/texas-transgender-sports-law/; Ken Paxton, Attorney General of Texas, "Opinion No. KP-0401: Re: Whether certain medical procedures performed on children constitute child abuse (RQ-0426-KP)," February 18, 2022, https://texasattorneygeneral.gov/sites/default/files/

global/KP-0401.pdf; "Mapping Attacks on LGBTQ Rights in U.S. State Legislatures," ACLU, last updated May 19, 2023, https://www.aclu.org/legislative-attacks-on-lgbtq-rights.

16. Austin Independent School District, "Cultivating Austin ISD's Equity Ecosystem," accessed August 2023, https://www.austinisd.org/equityoffice.

17. Unfortunately, this real-world challenge happened in Virginia in 2018, when a trans student was left in a hallway during an active shooter drill; see Tim Fitzsimons, "Virginia school allegedly barred trans student from active-shooter drill," *NBC News*, October 9, 2018.

Include

"Assume that there are trans adults and young people in every space that has adults and young people. That's something that seems to limit the thinking of a lot of people that I work with, the idea that yes, every, every trans student is going to be different in terms of their needs. But also, you need to anticipate having trans students in the first place, even if you don't know who they are, even if you never know who they are, you still need to be doing that work."
—Sam Long (he/him), high school science teacher in Denver

CLOSE YOUR eyes and think back to the first time you felt yourself reflected within a book, movie, song, or other creative work. What made that connection so strong? How did it feel? What was it like to see yourself (or, at least, a part of yourself) represented in someone else's work?

For those of us who are part of majority or privileged populations in the United States—men, white people, those who are neurotypical and/or able-bodied, Christians, straight people, and more—we see people "like us" in creative works (and in classroom curriculum) all the time, so much so that we often don't even notice. For example, the coauthors of this book are both white. As children, there were lots of picture books depicting people with skin like ours, and we saw people "like us" on television and in films. Even BAND-AIDs matched our skin tone.

For members of marginalized or minority populations, however, finding community or identity representation in media (or in classroom curriculum) is often more difficult. Throughout the entire 20th century, fewer than one in ten nominees for the Academy Awards was Black. Similarly, as recently as 2021, fewer than 4% of regularly appearing characters in scripted television shows had some sort of disability—and this low percentage was still a historic high. Meanwhile, one 2015 report found that women made up less than 20% of the experts featured in news stories and only 37% of reporters telling stories globally. With all that in mind, depicting diversity is crucial to marginalized and minority populations so that *all* members of our society can see themselves reflected in the world around them.[1]

But highlighting and showcasing diversity—in classroom content, curricula, posters on school walls, in school communications, and beyond—is not only important to those from underrepresented populations, it's also important to the entire school community. Chapter 5: Affirm is about supporting individual transgender and non-binary students; this section is about including transgender and non-binary identity and representation across an entire education community, in its culture, values, and how that community represents itself both internally and externally.

Trans Joy

Gender euphoria is a very important word. So a lot of times in the trans community, we talk about and have a focus on gender dysphoria, and how we have a disconnect from between our minds and our bodies or our minds and how other people perceive us. And gender euphoria is a feeling of alignment, a feeling of the way that people are interacting with me makes me feel visible, it makes me feel seen, makes me feel heard, makes me feel valid.

—Prin Ocea (they/them)[2]

Windows and Mirrors

In education spaces, this concept—that students both need to see themselves represented in curriculum and have opportunities to learn about others—is talked about as ensuring that student education includes both windows and mirrors: mirrors, so that students can learn about and better understand themselves and who they are, and windows, so that students can gain exposure to and learn about the experiences of others who may not be like them.[3] Some educators have expanded the concept of windows and mirrors to also include sliding glass doors, which allow readers to step into and inhabit someone else's experience rather than simply view it from afar.[4]

We spoke with Julie Stivers (she/her)—a school librarian in Raleigh, North Carolina, and 2023 School Library Journal National School Librarian of the Year—who described it this way:

> As the librarian, we're hitting everybody, and we're controlling so much of the narrative of stories that get told [to students]. So decisions we make or do not make have such a lasting impact or ripple effect throughout the school. Librarians, more than any other position, we have to have been doing internal work, we have to know what culturally sustaining pedagogy is,[5] we have to be operating in that way. We have to recognize the healing effects that an inclusive school space can have on students who have experienced homophobia and racism and transphobia.
>
> I have really high expectations for librarians. We are not gatekeepers of books. Instead, we should be equity leaders in our school. And that doesn't mean just leading PD, that means modeling with our students. Our collections should be so reflective [of our students] and so inclusive. But more than that, we should be trying to push reflective materials into the curriculum by any means necessary.

In many school communities, there is a distinct lack of both windows and mirrors (let alone sliding glass doors) around transgender and non-binary identity. That is, transgender and non-binary youth don't find their identities or experiences represented in existing curricula or school culture, and their cisgender peers aren't learning about trans and non-binary identities and experiences—and the importance of respecting those identities—either.

This lack of windows and mirrors is especially true for intersecting and overlapping minority or marginalized identities and life experiences, such as transgender and non-binary students of color, those with physical disabilities or who are neurodivergent, immigrants, non-Christian faith traditions, and more.

In our interview with transgender student Daniel Trujillo (he/him), he and his mom noted the first time he ever saw LGBTQ identity represented in a classroom; he was in 8th grade:

DANIEL: Last year we had a lesson based around learning the amendments. She [the teacher] taught the lesson about 14th amendment and Title IX; she taught the lesson from the viewpoint of a queer person who is getting bullied, and she showed this whole documentary about it.

At the beginning she gave us a handout, like a little preview quiz: Like what do you know about the amendments? Do you think these amendments protect everyone's rights? Do you think marginalized communities—like the LGBTQ community or people of color—are 100% protected by these rights?

Then, right before we watched the documentary, she did a presentation that was like, this is the percentages of people that are bullied and in schools, like a PSA, I think, 'cuz she was hearing like a lot of kids were saying stuff, like homophobic stuff, outside the classrooms. But it was really amazing seeing a lesson based around that kind of topic, which was cool. She actually talked about the LGBTQ civil rights movement.

LIZETTE,   And Daniel ran in to the car and was, like,
DANIEL'S   "I've never seen myself represented in the les-
MOM: son plan before!" He was really excited. I was impressed and thrilled!

FIGURE 6.1   Art twink, We Survive So We Can Thrive, 2023.[6]

Inclusive Education Communities

Fortunately, this lack of representation and understanding around trans and non-binary identities—and, indeed, around many minority and marginalized identities and life experiences—is slowly changing. As noted in the Introduction, there is increasing evidence that visible support for and inclusion of LGBTQ identities has a positive impact on all students, not just those who are LGBTQ.

Likewise, more and more education organizations—as well as individual educators—are working to change this lack of representation and to elevate the need for identity-conscious curriculum and instruction.

One such organization is the National Board for Professional Teaching Standards (NBPTS), which offers National Board Certification, the highest certification a teacher may obtain. From its inception in 1989, National Board Certification has focused not only on understanding and being able to teach general content, but on knowing who your students are and how to teach them as individuals. This implicitly ties to concepts of diversity, equity, and inclusion, as NBPTS teaching standards require educators to focus on what each student needs, rather than focus on an educator's feelings or beliefs around a particular topic or identity.

We spoke with Dr. Kristin Hamilton (she/her), a National Board Certified Teacher (NBCT) and Vice President of Standards and Assessment as NBPTS, about why the organization is so focused on ensuring that National Board Certified Teachers are creating inclusive education environments.

How is social/emotional learning integrated into the work that you're doing?

When the national board started in the '90s, it started out with adopting the five core propositions of what all teachers should know and be able to do. Those are common across content and grade level; those were adopted in 1989.

[AUTHOR'S NOTE: The National Board's Five Core Propositions are:

1. Teachers are committed to students and their learning.
2. Teachers know the subjects they teach and how to teach those subjects to students.
3. Teachers are responsible for managing and monitoring students learning.
4. Teachers think systematically about their practice and learn from experience.
5. Teachers are members of learning communities.]

The first core proposition is that teachers are committed to students and their learning. And then it goes from there to say that they know the subjects they teach and how to teach those subjects to students. They manage and monitor student learning, which is where assessment and facilitation comes in, that they think systematically about their practice and learn from experience and that they're members of learning communities. Because that first core proposition of the National Board was basically, "you pay attention to the children in front of you who happened to be your students, you're committed to them." That means you have to know them, you have to understand them. The board very early on said, we expect every set of standards to explicitly attend to fairness, equity, and diversity. And the National Board convened educators who could establish what we needed to see to say a practice is accomplished. Very early on, the definition of diversity was intended to provoke people to pay attention to aspects of identity that might otherwise be easy to just not pay attention to if you're not part of that community.

How would gender identity show up in the National Board's standards?

Because the way the assessment is designed, it's designed to not be overly prescriptive. It's designed to be responsive to the students who were in front of the teacher. So first, it's going to depend on performance-based assessments and is going to depend on who the students are. So for example, if in the context a teacher is explaining, "I understand all of this about my students, this is who they are," they're expected to show that they're attending to the range of what diversity is.

So if it's a particularly superficial understanding of who their students are, that might be one piece of evidence that starts to make that entry look less accomplished against the rubrics. Perhaps there's a mismatch, maybe the teacher is talking about identities and talking about identities and is seeing the range, the gorgeousness of who the students are in front of them, but there's a mismatch in the instruction.

What do you see as the value of this work for teachers who (rightly or wrongly) don't think they're working with diverse student bodies?

The value is tremendous! That's one of those sentences that we hear: "I don't have diversity [in my classroom]." Yes, you do! It might just not be showing up racially, or, you know, in other ways that are just completely visible. So while what you do might be different here or there, based on what's happening in your community, based on the needs of your students or what you're seeing in your professional learning community with your colleagues, regardless, an accomplished teacher should know and be aware of racial history in the United States, and how that impacts their school, their local context and how that's affecting their instruction. They should know how the needs of LGBTQIA+ students are, the challenges they face, how schools can support them. Even if I don't have students with a particular need today, it doesn't mean you won't tomorrow. That's how the standards address this.

Committees of practitioners we recently convened determined that National Board Standards will advance and see significant revisions in such areas as affirming gender identities and all LGBTQIA+ communities, teacher and student belonging and self-care, social/emotional learning, inclusion and belonging, trauma informed practice, . . . all of those pieces.

What thoughts or advice might you have for educators in places pushing anti-LGBTQ+ laws or policies?

I can tell you right now the national board's position is never going to be "well, there's nothing you can do." The national board's position also can't be that, in order to be board certified, you have to do exactly these three things in any situation. That's not skillful, and part of being an accomplished practitioner is being skillful and understanding your context.

A teacher may say, "I have the student in need here. I have these trans students who are being harmed. Maybe I have a trans colleague who's being harmed." Because of the beauty of the five core propositions—I attend to myself, I attend to my colleagues, I attend to my students—it's not okay to do nothing. We know that it would be possible for two accomplished teachers in the same situation to make different choices. But we do have an obligation to establish expectations that you do *something*.

Our revision committees of practitioners will help define, "these are your considerations, these are the non-negotiables. This is where you're going to have to be deft and skillful. This is where it's up to you." This is where an accomplished teacher looks to determine if it was enough, if it worked, what you're going to do differently. But you're not off the hook there, you're not done, just because you did one thing.

First and foremost, you're obligated to be committed to your students. And you have to know who they are. You can't pretend you don't see certain things and be upholding core proposition one at the same time. It's impossible.

Curricular organizations and professional associations are having similar conversations about the need for inclusive educational environments. The National Council for the Social Studies (NCSS), for example, identified a number of important themes in advance of the organization's 2023 conference, including one that explicitly mentions LGBTQ inclusion:

> Inclusive Social Studies—Who Are We? The intent of this sub-theme is to help teach a more comprehensive history that includes multiple perspectives to help students and educators better understand the complexities of humanity. [Including] elevating historically marginalized voices: BIPOC, LGBTQIA+, SPED, ELL, indigenous peoples, refugees, immigrants, disabled persons, other marginalized groups.[7]

Finally, both the American Association of School Librarians (AASL) and the American Library Association (ALA) have resources and professional standards that speak to the importance of creating inclusive learning environments, even as libraries and librarians are increasingly being targeted by anti-LGBTQ rhetoric and political pressure.

The ALA has a dedicated webpage stating that libraries should "serve LGBTQIA+ people by ensuring that this population is reflected in library collections and provided with services at the library." Likewise, the ALA's Code of Ethics speaks to the need for libraries that "advance racial and social justice," among other things:

> We affirm the inherent dignity and rights of every person. We work to recognize and dismantle systemic and individual biases; to confront inequity and oppression; to enhance diversity and inclusion; and to advance racial and social justice in our libraries, communities, profession, and associations through awareness, advocacy, education, collaboration, services, and allocation of resources and spaces.[8]

Meanwhile, the AASL focuses on six "shared foundations": inquire, include, collaborate, curate, explore, and engage. The "include" foundation encourages school librarians to "start with equity" and to "build a collection that reflects the diverse global community."[9] Librarian Julie Stivers literally wrote the book on AASL's "include" foundation, available as part of the AASL's *National School Library Standards* series; when Stivers spoke with us she noted "the expectation [as a librarian] going into a school space, my job is to welcome every student and disrupt when I see things that aren't working."

AASL has also cosponsored Jazz & Friends National Day of School & Community Readings, an annual program that "invites communities across the country . . . to advocate for the rights of transgender and non-binary youth and ensure that every child has the support needed to thrive and be their whole self in their school and community."[10]

As evidenced from these examples, those leading the charge in education know that inclusion, social justice, and ethical education must include all students, and indeed all people, not just those in the majority or with privileged identities or experiences.

Creating Inclusive Classrooms and Curricula

"There are times when children reveal more about themselves, and they're leading the space in a way that they are not typically in the rest of the day. They get to explore their own creativity. That is where we see gender-bendy kids bringing their full selves out. And a really great teacher is going to be able to ask them questions in an appropriate way about that, to lead classroom conversations about what we learn together when we play dress up. What are we learning about the ways we can be in the world, and how did we treat each other when some of us chose costumes that maybe others of us weren't expecting?

"That is a different orientation for teaching that is more about facilitating experiences that are not highly controlled, but allow children to bring more of their full selves into the classroom. I'm really interested in strengthening teachers' skills to be able to do that, so that they are really good at listening to kids, really get it or observing kids, and then developing responsive curriculum from that listening and observation. It sounds like it's not as neat and tidy as saying, 'get their pronouns right, get their names right,' but it's a much more fundamental issue."

—Dr. Harper Keenan, Assistant Professor in the Department of Curriculum & Pedagogy at the University of British Columbia Faculty of Education; founder of the Trans Educators Network (TEN)

When creating inclusive classrooms and curricula for trans and non-binary students, it can be easy to address surface-level issues—like names and pronouns—without more deeply rethinking curricula or classroom structure. That isn't to say names and pronouns are unimportant, but that a truly inclusive education environment goes so much deeper than *just* names and pronouns. Likewise, while the authors of this book can give advice on what trans students may want or need in general, only your students can tell you their specific needs and priorities.

First and foremost, consider your role in supporting students and what you can do to ensure that all students have access to, and confidence in, learning core standards. Knowing how to make both lessons and curricula tied to those standards and inclusive of diverse identities is critical and can allow for some outside-the-box thinking. Organizations like Welcoming Schools and GLSEN have numerous other resources for classroom teachers as well, and you may even be able to search online for "trans inclusive curriculum on _____" to find existing lesson plans or curriculum guides for specific topics and grade levels. For a list of specific curricular resources, see Appendix 1: Additional Resources.

To understand how teachers can create inclusive classroom libraries, we spoke with Jessica Cisneros (she/her), a veteran educator and instructional coach who is well known for her innovative classroom spaces. She has spent her career teaching and coaching in Washington, DC.

Why did you want to/need to create an inclusive library for your class? What was the impetus?

I grew up as a multi-racial Latinx child in the south and by the time I was in high school, I had become aware and unhappy about the fact that I had never read a single Latinx author in school, never had a single class that focused on Latin America, never really saw myself reflected in anything we learned about in school. I was determined that my students would see themselves in my classroom, that they would have affirming representation in the books we read, the lessons we engaged in and on the walls of the classroom.

By my third year of teaching, I had experienced some biases held by a colleague around gender expression—notably with regard to children who didn't conform to expected gender norms. I pushed back against these biases and began to think more about how to incorporate gender-inclusive books in our classroom. I had heard students say things like "pink is for girls!" many times and knew that there were a lot of ingrained stereotypes and beliefs that I could work to combat in the classroom.

Having a transgender student one year when I was teaching kindergarten was a catalyst in understanding the ways I had previously come up short in creating a truly gender-inclusive classroom. That year I explored many children's books that incorporated themes of gender expansiveness, non-binary views of gender, transgenderism and beyond. I learned things I hadn't known I didn't know.

How did you go about finding a grant/paying for the books?

The grant we applied for was very open-ended, open to anyone who could demonstrate that this grant would help to support the local community (in this case, Capitol Hill, Washington, DC). Here is a snippet from our grant proposal:

> We believe that classroom libraries should be both a window and a mirror to students. A window to the world of diversity and a mirror that reflects their own identities. We are

proposing a project to create classroom libraries at Two Rivers that reflect both family and gender diversity and affirmation. Representation in children's books matters and studies show that students who are shown positive representations of other people are more likely to be accepting of others. We believe this will contribute to increased kindness, inclusiveness, and understanding in our classrooms and communities. We are asking for support in the form of funds to purchase these books and we will offer our expertise to help to train teachers at Two Rivers to use the books to effectively launch discussions about diversity, gender and stereotypes and kindness/inclusivity.

What went into choosing the books in your library?

Many hours of research! We reviewed many book lists from trusted sources like HRC Welcoming Schools and Gender Spectrum. We chose books to reflect a variety of themes and grade levels, and we tried to create some basic guidance for fellow teachers about how to utilize these books.[11]

Why do you think it's important for students, especially students with many intersecting identities (including trans and non-binary) to see themselves in books? Why is it important for those without those identities to read about them?

Students are in schools for a significant percentage of their waking hours. To not see yourself reflected in the classroom is to feel invisible, unacknowledged, and unseen. From working with students for 20 years, I have realized that all students want to be seen, affirmed, and loved for who they are (much like adults . . .).

This is something we have to work actively for because the world is set up to do the opposite. Anytime I am searching for clipart for the classroom, for example, it takes a lot more effort to find nonwhite children in clipart online. In a thousand small ways, a teacher can accidentally affirm stereotypes and biased views of gender, race, and a slew of other identities. We know students receive these biased messages in myriad ways and we have to work to show them a different possibility.

I had a moment of realization at one point after the experience of having a transgender child in my classroom. That year the school had supported me in purchasing several books to make sure that our classroom library featured transgender characters and people from history that were part of the LGBTQ community. However none of these materials had been purchased for other classrooms—it was thought that my classroom needed these books but that was only doing part of what needed to be done. In reality, all students should be "meeting" all types of people in their class library. All students at our school would meet, know, interact with transgender people in our community so it made no sense that they would also not get to meet transgender folks in the literary world.

Have you had to deal with push-back on books about gender identity? If so, what did you do? If not, what would you do/say?

Teaching at a school of choice with a supportive administration, we were upfront about the fact that we considered teaching utilizing books about gender inclusivity were non-negotiable and a part of who we were as a school. There were two occasions when families elected to leave with varying levels of candidness about their reasoning, but both seemed related to this issue.

I think responding to parent concerns is about showing how teaching about gender inclusiveness really just means we are teaching about people and about care for community and for each other.

One of my favorite memories of teaching is when one of my parents thanked me for doing things she didn't know to ask for—like having a windows and mirrors type of classroom library. It was so rewarding to see both that I could do that for her child and also that she forever after would know to ask and push for this if she wasn't seeing it in her child's classroom.

But creating inclusive classrooms and curricula doesn't need to be limited to classroom libraries. Sam Long (he/him) is a transgender educator in Colorado. In addition to his teaching and advocacy, he had delved full force into examining his biology curriculum and developing a framework for gender-inclusive biology. Through his content expertise and life experience, he developed the framework of "Authenticity, Continuity, Affirmation, Anti-Oppression and Student Agency," which he found allowed him to create lessons and learning experiences for students to understand the complexities of gender and sexuality as natural variations. The full framework is in online version Bonus Resource 5.

Tell us about your gender-inclusive science curriculum. What makes it unique? What have you changed?

I started thinking about what changes are needed in the canonical biology curriculum, and something that came up was the fact that the traditional ways of teaching biology in middle and high school are over-simplified. One of the areas in which they're overly simplified is anything about gender, sex, and sexuality. They often would say things that in middle and high school, you might teach, but if you go any further and understand science, you're gonna realize it is not true. Saying that "humans have chromosomes, and people have either XX or XY, and that's what makes you a man or a woman." Statements like, "In evolution, every individual needs to reproduce. That's the main measure of your fitness and your success as individuals: to reproduce."

FIGURE 6.2   Liberal Jane Illustration, If Your Activism isn't Accessible and Inclusive, Who is it Even For?, 2023.[12]

And those are things that overgeneralize, in middle and high school, and they don't really serve trans students well (among a lot of other students) because they don't acknowledge that gender is different from sex, and they don't acknowledge that somebody's identity might not match what is being taught. So my first attempts were in the first year teaching, to add little things or to change language to improve the impact of those lessons.

There was a lesson about chromosomes where you were supposed to research intersex traits, but they were being called by very outdated names, and they're also being called diseases instead of just traits. So I changed that language. One of the first things I did is mentioned to [students] that the generalizations that we see here are generalizations, and that people are a lot more diverse than this. That's where the curriculum needs to improve. I didn't know how far I would end up taking that, but it turned out that there were a lot of things in the curriculum that needed changing. And there were at least some students in that first year that told me right away that they appreciated the fact that I acknowledged the shortcomings of the curriculum.

That's how I started thinking about gender-inclusive biology. And then I made more changes and tried out more things for a couple of years. And then, after, after those couple of years, I got in touch with [fellow teachers] Lewis [Steller] and River [Suh], we started the project website, which now gives a lot more detailed guidance on how to teach about genetics in a way that is accurate to all people's identities and is accurate to species other than humans, guidance on how to teach about biodiversity and evolution in a way that doesn't overgeneralize about the role of reproduction, about parenting and sexual behavior and the fact that those are different things, and that they all are facets of any species behavior. We have similar guidance about anatomy and how to talk about bodies and patterns and bodies without overgeneralizing and well, giving all the students the accurate knowledge that they would need. So we try to align it with what the better medical schools and professional schools are doing in terms of preparing their students to work with actual clients.

And you developed a framework for gender inclusion in the biology curriculum?

The framework for gender-inclusive biology has five parts, none of which are really specific to biology, or to teaching about gender. The first is authenticity, which is about teaching what is based on evidence and teaching the full truth as soon as possible.

Then is continuity, teaching things that are consistent with what you're going to teach the next day, rather than teaching generalizations and then having to go back and patch up, or acknowledge (or ignore) the fact that you've taught something that's not correct. And embedding the content rather than having just a "very special lesson" at the end of a period of study.

The third part of the framework is affirmation. Whenever possible, we discuss variations in living things as interesting, positive, and worth learning about rather than weird, bizarre, exceptional, all things that are done a lot in medicine.

Then there is anti-oppression, the need to acknowledge systems of power and harm in historical and current practices and science.

Student agency tells us to include students in the process of choosing what they want to learn about, or focus on. And in giving very continual feedback on what the way that we're teaching is doing for them, whether it's supporting them or they need something different, because students want to learn about what's relevant to them. This is especially important in a science class, when you're saying this science class has the ability to be relevant to your identity and your community and to make sense in the context outside of science. Students really appreciate that and they want to have a say in what that looks like.

What kind of response have you seen from students, from educator peers, from parents or community, and from school administration?

What is different about this type of teaching is that we're usually acknowledging at the beginning of a period of study how the things that we're learning are related to the people that are doing the learning and doing the science. For example, we might be in a genetics unit and I say, "We are going to learn about genetics. We're going to learn part of what makes us who we are as humans, and the diversity within humans. We're going to need to talk about gender identity because we're going to be looking at chromosomes, and we need to say what they are and what they aren't, in terms of what they make us." If there's a student that isn't trans or hasn't thought about this before, it's going to build on what they've learned in middle school science, but it's going to change the way that they talk about genetics.

And then for students that might be thinking about this, or maybe they've felt in the past, "We're learning about something that really doesn't involve me," or "it's so overgeneralized that it doesn't include my experience'," now they realize things are different in this class, and those students might be able to help other students to engage more and be more part of the learning.

I see students that traditionally do not participate a lot in science, but really care about talking about social issues and social studies. And if we're talking about gender inclusion, sometimes those students will be leaders of those discussions, and I'll hear from them a lot more. And [for] some students, it affects them but they don't want to talk about it because they don't want to draw attention to themselves. So what I'll see from some of them is not necessarily more outward participation, but I see them look up or be more engaged.

The response from parents or families, if they hear about what we're learning about in school, has generally been positive. Sometimes, if the response is not positive, a parent or guardian would talk to someone else [on staff] besides me. Once we did a lesson about reproductive strategies, and some of the examples were the clownfish—when one of them dies, the other one changes its sex—and some lizards that were living in an all-female colony, but are stealing sperm from other lizards. I think one student went home and the parent asked "Well, what did you do today?" And she said, "We learned about transgender fish." The parent emailed me saying, "I didn't know that this was in the curriculum." So I sent her the whole lesson plan and I didn't hear back. It seemed to me that the parents' concern was no longer the same once she saw what the lesson was about.

There's this idea—and it makes me think of a lot of the things we've seen with journalism the last couple of years as well—that there's "objective science teacher," who, of course, has no racial identity or gender identity or sexual orientation or physical disability or neurodivergence because all of those things are atypical. You end up with this desire for a so-called "neutral" science teacher, which is really just reinforcing white cisgender Christian, straight, able-bodied, neurotypical ideas. That's never been true. There's never been "neutrality" in science or "objectivity" in science. We just need to be honest about what we're bringing to the table.

FIGURE 6.3   Liberal Jane Illustration, Inclusive Curriculums Benefit All Students, 2023.[13]

We spoke with Dave (he/him) and Hannah (she/her) Edwards, parents of a trans child and advocates for trans rights, about finding resources for creating inclusive classrooms. Dave is also the CEO of Gender Inclusive Schools and a national facilitator with Human Rights Campaign's Welcoming Schools, while Hannah is the training coordinator at OutFront Minnesota, an LGBTQ advocacy organization, and the director of Transforming Families, a Minnesota organization for parents and caregivers of trans youth. Dave and Hannah said:

> We love the resource from Welcoming Schools called Developing a Gender Inclusive School.[14] It talks about having conversations that help get kids on the same page, and also how to respond to kids who have questions or who might say, "Well, my dad says boys can't wear dresses."
>
> I think, you know, the Mama Bear teacher in me wants to say, "Christopher, stop being so mean," but there are students who legitimately have that question, and maybe it's coming from a place where they're seeing this for the first time. Maybe they're connecting with it, right? Maybe they're too scared to talk about it at home. So it's good to remind yourself that that's also a possibility. With resources like Welcoming Schools, you get that practice. So it's not something you're having to think about in the moment.
>
> Welcoming Schools also encourages educators in the trainings to get with their grade level teams and calendar out their lesson plans. Maybe something bad happened and now they need to fix harm that was caused, and part of that is saying "every first-grade teacher is going to read this book during this week," and then replicating that over the course of the year. That can be really powerful.
>
> I also ask educators to think about what if a student now is in fifth grade, and they've had four years of these calendared-out equity books and lesson plans and conversations, think of all the different kinds of people and families they're going to know about and have as background knowledge before they moved to middle school. What a cool thing to be able to keep working towards. That proactive piece is what I ask people to focus on the most.

Beyond that, at least for elementary school, it's really just about noticing and highlighting awesome aspects of someone's identity when it occurs. So in current events, or if they're learning about an artist or a scientist, really not ignoring any parts of their identities but really holding them up. And that's true for any kind of identity.

Creating inclusive classrooms is also an opportunity to practice "I Do, We Do, You Do" teaching strategies, in which the teacher demonstrates a practice (e.g., "I'm introducing myself with my name and pronouns"), asks students to work through examples together (e.g., "we go through a chapter of the reading and discuss the gender and pronouns of the characters"), and finally has students demonstrate their new skill (e.g., "you share your thoughts on a character's gender with the class").

Trans Joy

It meant so much to me, when I would see people being visibly queer and trans. So that gives me the courage sometimes to be visibly queer and trans. Because I think maybe someone will see me that needs to see that.

—Ashlee Craft (they/them)[15]

Wesley Hedgepeth (he/him) is the President of the National Council for the Social Studies, and a politics and history teacher at Collegiate School in Henrico County, Virginia. He told us that, at its best, school should allow students to think beyond their own experiences, and consider how they can take action in larger world:

The guardrails we provide students with in the school environment provide students guidance while they practice inquiry and 'do social studies'. It's crucial to

practice this in a safe classroom setting. This equips
students to continue 'doing social studies' outside,
such as researching solutions to problems in their
communities or discussing issues they care about with
neighbors.

A history or government class, for instance,
might analyze policy statements made by the Lyndon
B. Johnson presidential campaign. Students could
then generate and answer compelling questions,
such as: To what extent did domestic public opinion
shape the U.S. military and political strategies during
the Vietnam War? They could then act upon their
learning, which could be a class presentation. Another
topic such as LGBTQ+ rights might segue into
advocacy, enabling students to leverage their newfound
knowledge in championing causes that matter to them.

Things to Consider in Elementary Classrooms

- Use books with transgender and non-binary characters to
  teach lessons about plot, characters, and setting. All children's books have these critical pieces, and using inclusive
  texts will do double duty on representation and standards.

  - You can always mix up gendered language for existing
    texts, too, for example, by re-writing the *Three Little Pigs* so
    that not all the pigs are boys.

- Find free inclusive texts and lesson plans from organizations
  like Welcoming Schools or Pride and Less Prejudice.[16]

  - An example of the *Calvin* lesson plan is in online version
    Bonus Resource 7.

- When discussing bodies, gender expression, and language,
  be sure to ask students about the "rules" they may see in
  the world (e.g., that boys have short hair and girls have
  long hair; boys shouldn't cry; girls shouldn't like sports,
  etc.) and use those discussions as opportunities for learning
  and growth.

- For math, trans advocate Gavin Grimm suggested using writing word problems that are inclusive of various identities and family relationships. Instead of "My mom went to the store to buy 8 eggs, 3 cartons of milk, and a bag of sugar; how many items did my mom buy?" Consider shifting to my "My maddy" or "My two moms."[17]

Things to Consider in Middle School Classrooms

- For all students, emphasize that they are the experts in their bodies and experiences, but shouldn't be attempting to enforce spoken or unspoken gender roles or rules on anyone else.

- Use discussion questions to address gender stereotyping, rather than simply saying that a gender stereotype is incorrect. For example, if a student says "boys can't do ballet" or "girls can't play football," discuss where they learned those ideas and why they might be true or false, rather than directly telling a student that they're wrong.

- Books continue to be a central piece of the puzzle for creating an inclusive middle school. Consider applying to the GLSEN Rainbow Library for a set of books and lesson plans aligned to middle school standards.[18]

- In math, start looking at population percentages and ratios and identify where marginalized folks such as transgender people are appearing, growing, or changing.

- In history, talk about transgender and non-binary historical and modern-day figures, and how support for trans communities has changed over time.

Things to Consider in High School Classrooms

- Consider "social justice math" as a way to introduce LGBTQ and other identity-related issues in math curricula. For example, students might learn about ratios to explore social divisions or the presence of in-groups and out-groups in a culture or society.[19]

- Have students create personal narratives about their intersecting identities (at levels that feel comfortable) in the form of a genre of choice.

- Use examples from the real world—both history and current events—as entry points to discuss students' beliefs about gender and how to treat each other with respect.

Trans-Inclusive Health and Sex Education

"Health education is vital to the primary mission of schools. Research demonstrates important connections between health and learning and highlights the critical role of schools in providing coordinated and comprehensive health education for all students. Health education helps youth gain the functional knowledge and skills needed for making health promoting decisions, achieving health literacy, adopting health-enhancing behaviors, and promoting the health of others. Health education tends to be more effective when delivered by well-trained and supported educators, given adequate instructional time and resources, and when it incorporates linkages to other school curricular areas."
—Profiles 2020: School Health Profiles[20]

For health and sex education to be truly inclusive of trans and non-binary students, instruction must cover more than reproduction and sexually transmitted infections. While most secondary schools require that students take some sort of health education, only 2 out of every 5 lead health education teachers received professional development on how to support LGBTQ students. Some states even require health education that explicitly discriminates against LGBTQ students, such as by claiming that children are best raised by a man and a woman, or that being part of the LGBTQ community inherently puts people at higher risk for disease or other negative health outcomes.[21]

In our interview with Armonte Butler (he/him), Associate Director of LGBT Health and Rights at Advocates for Youth in Washington, DC, he noted that creating inclusive health and sex ed curriculum requires "ensuring young people see and review it and express what feels right to them." Advocates for Youth "partners with young people and their adult allies to champion youth rights to bodily autonomy and build power to transform policies, programs and systems to secure sexual health and equity for all youth."[22] This includes creating and training educators and education systems to adopt comprehensive and inclusive sex education.

Butler described the organization's "Three Rs" (rights, respect, and responsibility) as key to its work:

> We believe that young people have the right to medically accurate information in sex education. We believe that young people have the right to honest education.
>
> We also believe young people should be treated with respect, so anything that we work on—whether it's a paper or a presentation or a training—we push out to young people. I've seen them get their hands on it, to really ensure that they're included on issues that are related to them or about them.
>
> Then the last R is responsibility. We believe that adults have a responsibility to provide young people with opportunities to develop partnerships, the responsibility to ensure that adults are providing youth with these tools and resources.
>
> Inclusive sex education is lifesaving for young people, especially trans and non-binary youth. By offering honest, medically accurate, and inclusive sex education, schools are safer, and young people from all backgrounds are healthier. Inclusive sex education is associated with improved health and reduces the chances of stigma experienced by trans and non-binary

> youth. The lack of inclusive sex education fuels hos-
> tile school environments and often promotes preju-
> dice against trans and non-binary youth. Trans and
> non-binary youth experience severe health disparities
> due to the lack of tools and resources like inclusive
> sex education which would increase their knowledge
> and awareness about health, sexuality, and STI
> prevention.[23]

Unfortunately, the CDC found that more than half of states saw some level of decrease in health and sex ed programs between 2010 and 2020, either in the amount of instruction offered, the topics included in that instruction, or the resources available to students outside the classroom.[24] That decrease, coupled with the rise in the number of students identifying as transgender or non-binary, means that educators must be especially mindful of what their students are learning in health and sex ed programming. Not only is less instruction happening, the instruction that is happening may be heteronormative and leave out LGBTQ identities and experiences.

Imagine the experience of a trans or non-binary student in a non-comprehensive program. One person we spoke with, the parent of a trans child in New England, in a state that is generally considered progressive, noted how far their child's sex education had to go:

> At this middle school, sex education was left to a
> single day in fifth grade—then a more comprehensive
> health curriculum that does *not* include sex education
> or gender conversations in sixth to eighth grade. Put
> yourself in the shoes of a fifth grader looking towards
> that single day program. The only puberty/sex-ed
> lesson happens one day a year, and a letter is sent
> home in advance. In this letter, it notes that "students
> who menstruate" will go in one classroom, while "stu-
> dents who do not menstruate" will go in another. The
> day will go over the basics of puberty by sub-group.

Where does our non-binary student go? Where does a transgender girl go? By these definitions, if both were assigned male at birth, they'd go to the "non-menstruating group" but how would that make the transgender girl feel? For the non-binary student, they are being forced to "choose a side" when neither may feel true to their reality and identity. Inclusive and comprehensive sex education takes all of this into account and ensures a holistic, student-centered approach.

One of the authors of this book remembers her high school sex ed class being divided into girls, who went to hear from a guest speaker about breast cancer, and boys, who went to hear from a guest speaker about testicular cancer. Putting aside the problematic assumptions—that all students can easily be put into "boy" or "girl" groups and that everyone in the 'girl' group would develop breasts and that everyone in the 'boy' group had testicles—this type of sex segregation also implies that girls shouldn't learn about testicular cancer and boys shouldn't learn about breast cancer.

Like many areas of education policy, some places are changing for the better and some for the worse. For example, seven states now require instruction that "include affirming sexual orientation instruction on LGBQT identities or discussion of sexual health for LGBQT youth," a positive trend that may continue, but 35 states still require "schools to stress abstinence when sex education or HIV/STI instruction is provided."[25]

When pushing for comprehensive health and sex education in your school education community, it's important to stress that comprehensive sex ed is age-appropriate and ensures that all students (and their communities and families) are supported and included.

Simple Things You Can Do

Organizations like GLSEN, Advocates for Youth, and Gender-Inclusive Biology all have teaching and curricular resources available for a range of grades and ages, the specifics of which are beyond the scope of this book. That said, there are a few simple things any teacher can do (whether or not they're teaching health or sex ed!) to be more inclusive of trans and non-binary students:

- Tie things back to your school's mission and values. If you have concerns about pushback or negative responses to inclusive language and curriculum, you can always connect back to the mission and value of your school, and the importance of providing students with accurate and up-to-date information.

- Affirm the existence of LGBTQ people. When discussing the range of human experience, be sure to include examples that are not all straight and cis. When focusing on health and sex ed, define and explain terms like asexual, non-binary, intersex, and all the other language covered in the Glossary.

- Teach with "people who have . . ." language. Rather than saying "women can get breast cancer" or "men can get testicular cancer," say "people with breasts can get breast cancer" or "people with testicles can get testicular cancer." While this type of language can take some getting used to, it ensures that students are being taught specific and scientifically accurate language.

Creating Inclusive Extracurricular Activities

Not all learning or student activities happen during the school day. Extracurriculars are often just as much a part of a student's school experience as math and science, and may make or break a trans or non-binary student's experience at school.

In general, trans and non-binary students should receive the same support and affirmation in extracurriculars as they do in the classroom. This includes relatively simple things like names and pronouns, as well as ensuring that programming and activities represent diverse student identities and experiences.

The School GSA

A school GSA (which used to stand for Gay-Straight Alliance and now often stands for Genders and Sexualities Alliance) is a key extracurricular for many trans and non-binary students. The specific structure and purpose of a GSA may vary from school to school—some may be more social, while others more activism-focused, some may be educational, while others may offer a way to connect with LGBTQ communities and resources outside of school—but the general purpose of any GSA is to provide a safe space for LGBTQ students *and allies* to come together and connect. This community and connection can be incredibly important, and the CDC found that GSAs tend to increase "school connectedness" for all students, not just those who are LGBTQ.[26]

The federal Equal Access Act of 1984 requires that schools receiving federal funding must treat all extracurricular clubs and programs equally; as long as the club or program does not interfere with the school's educational programming, schools can't pick and choose which clubs to allow and which to forbid. In practice, this means that if a school allows *any* extracurricular clubs or programs, the school must also allow GSAs. (Ironically, the Equal Access Act was originally lobbied for by Christian groups to ensure that schools could host extracurricular Bible study, but has more recently become a key tool in fighting for the right of students to organize GSAs.[28])

The ACLU has a resource on starting a GSA, available online at https://www.aclu.org/other/how-start-gay-straight-alliance-gsa. Key recommendations for students include:

1. Be able to explain why you want to start a GSA.
2. Find out your school's rules for setting up a club.

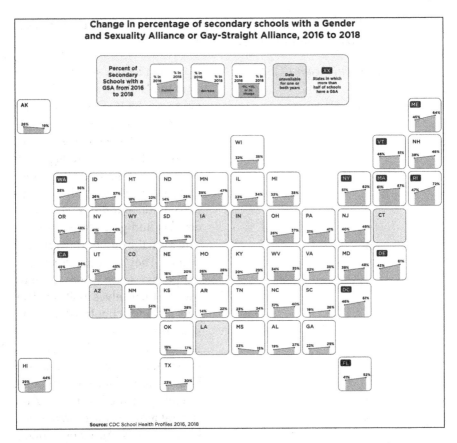

FIGURE 6.4   Child Trends, Only 9 States and DC Report That More Than Half of Secondary Schools Have a Gender and Sexuality Alliance, 2021.[27]

3. Find a faculty advisor or sponsor.

4. Tell the administration that you want to start a GSA.

5. Prepare and turn in any necessary paperwork.

The ACLU guide also has common arguments against GSAs and possible responses. For example:

Argument Against GSAs:	"We can't let our students have a club that's about sex."
Possible Response:	GSAs are NOT about sex. GSAs are about valuing all people regardless of whether they're gay, straight, bisexual, transgender, or questioning. Like any other club, GSAs offer students with a common interest a chance to connect and give students a respite from the day-to-day grind of school. They're about creating a supportive space where students can be themselves without fear and making schools safer for all students by promoting respect for everyone. A GSA meeting is no more about sex than the homecoming dance or any other school-sponsored activity. And several federal courts have ruled in favor of GSAs when schools have used this as an excuse to try to stop them from forming.

Student Athletics

As is discussed in Chapter 5: Affirm, school policies will ideally contain explicit language noting that trans students can participate in athletic programs that align with the student's gender identity, and that there should be no additional barriers to entry for trans or non-binary students. In practice, we know that trans participation student athletics can become a contentious and emotionally charged issue, and that laws, policies, and federal guidelines will likely have changed by the time this book goes to print. With that in mind, here are some helpful things to consider for any student athletic program:

- **What is the purpose of student athletics?** Student athletics are an opportunity for young people to learn teamwork, fair play, and how to win and lose gracefully. Allowing trans students to participate only builds upon those values, it doesn't detract from them.

- **Who gets to decide what is "fair"?** In sports, there are lots of things outside of our control that may impact who is better or worse at a particular activity. For example, in the 2021–2022 season, the average basketball player in the NBA was 8 inches taller than the average American male. Is that "unfair" to shorter people? Likewise, researchers found that Olympic swimmer Michael Phelps's "height, wingspan, and large hands and feet give him an advantage in swimming" and that his body "produces less lactic acid than his rivals, which shortens his recovery time."[29] Is his participation in swimming "unfair" to swimmers without those advantages? Why are those situations "fair," but it might be considered "unfair" for trans people to compete?

- **Sex verification testing in sports harms more than just trans people.** Many of the athletes subjected to invasive and humiliating "sex verification checks" are not transgender. Some states are even asking for the menstrual history of student athletes. Likewise, sex verification is disproportionately used to target women of color, adding an undercurrent of racism to sex testing for athletes.[30]

Trans Joy

I love playing with other boys on my baseball and basketball teams. I love being able to be who I am.

—Lil (he/him), 10

Other Things to Consider

Overnight Trips: When going on overnight trips, students may be required to stay in rooms with other students. Ideally, students should be able to select which of their peers they want to room with, but this may not always be possible. Overnight trips may be complicated by the fact that many camps or sleepaway facilities are set up with sex-segregated housing.

Above all, it's important not to force a trans or non-binary person to stay in a room that makes them uncomfortable, that forces them to bunk in a way that doesn't align with the student's identity, or to force them to bunk alone. (Bunking alone can be a great *option*, but no student should be required to do so.)

Student Theater: What would it look like to have gender-blind casting? This can be an opportunity to discuss gender, gender expression, and gender roles with students, rather than requiring students to conform to societal expectations.

Putting It into Practice

Following are scenarios to consider about addressing real-world challenges and personal reflection questions to ask yourself. We encourage you to take some time to reflect and catch your breath before taking action.

Personal Reflection Questions

1. What is your comfort with discussing gender with students? Colleagues? Parents? What can you do to increase your comfort?

2. As an educator, one of the most important things to do is look for the "ins." Where *in* the curriculum and standards could trans and non-binary people be represented? Where *in* the curriculum is content linked to gender and sexuality?

Where *in* the curriculum can you see the voices of trans and non-binary people? Consider your own roles and responsibilities, including any curriculum and standards. Where are the "ins"?

Addressing Real-World Challenges

1. What changes or adjustments might you need to make in your classroom or school more supportive of trans and non-binary students, even if there currently aren't any out trans or non-binary students?

2. Some of the vested parties in your community—colleagues, the school principal, parents—may strongly believe that talking about gender (and specifically talking about trans identity) is not appropriate in the classroom. How might you respond? What allies would you bring into the conversation? What resources would you share with the concerned parties?

3. Note that your responses to the preceding items might be different in an elementary school versus a middle school or a high school.

4. How can you support trans and non-binary students beyond the classroom curriculum? How do you think about common spaces like hallways or lunchrooms? What about extracurricular activities? How supportive is the broader community, outside of school?

5. Given your current role and situation, what real-world challenges does this section bring up for you in your community? How might you approach those challenges? What resources currently exist from your school/district/board of education to handle these challenges?

6. If your current role changed, how might your thoughts on these challenges change? Think about how you might answer differently as a classroom teacher, a school principal, a district administrator, and so on.

Notes

1. "These charts explain how Oscars diversity is way more complicated than you think," *Washington Post*, February 26, 2016, https://www.washingtonpost.com/news/arts-and-entertainment/wp/2016/02/26/these-charts-explain-how-oscars-diversity-is-way-more-complicated-than-you-think/; Lauren Appelbaum, "Percentage of characters with disabilities on TV reaches 11-Year record high," *RespectAbility*, January 14, 2021, https://www.respectability.org/2021/01/glaad-report-2020/; Aneeta Rattan, Siri Chilazi, Oriane Georgeac, and Iris Bohnet, "Tackling the underrepresentation of women in media," *Harvard Business Review*, June 6, 2019, https://hbr.org/2019/06/tackling-the-underrepresentation-of-women-in-media; Jo-Ann Finkelstein, "What's behind the magic of seeing yourself represented?" *Psychology Today*, January 19, 2021, https://www.psychologytoday.com/us/blog/demystifying-talk-therapy/202101/whats-behind-the-magic-seeing-yourself-represented.

2. Prin Ocea, quoted in Daylina Miller, "Trans joy: Putting the focus on gender euphoria," WUSF Public Media—WUSF 89.7, May 11, 2022, https://wusfnews.wusf.usf.edu/local-state/2022-05-11/trans-joy-putting-the-focus-on-gender-euphoria.

3. The specific language of "windows and mirrors" was developed by educator Emily Style in her 1988 paper "Curriculum as Window and Mirror."

4. Emily Style, "Curriculum as window and mirror," *Listening for All Voices*, Oak Knoll School monograph, Summit, NJ, 1988, republished by the National SEED Project, Wellesley Centers for Women, Wellesley College, n.d., https://nationalseedproject.org/Key-SEED-Texts/curriculum-as-window-and-mirror; WeAreTeachers Staff, "What Are Windows, Mirrors, and Sliding Glass Doors?," WeAreTeachers, Teacher Created Materials, July 12, 2018, https://www.weareteachers.com/mirrors-and-windows/.

5. Culturally Sustaining Pedagogy (CSP) is an approach to education that encourages students to celebrate and uplift their cultures and

identities, and for educators to build those cultures and identities into classroom material.

6. Art twink, We Survive So We Can Thrive, https://tdor.co/art/we-survive-so-we-can-thrive/.

7. "Call for Proposals: 103rd NCSS Annual Conference, Nashville, TN, December 1–3, 2023," National Council for the Social Studies, 2023, https://www.socialstudies.org/conference/proposals.

8. "Libraries respond: Services to LGBTQIA+ people," American Library Association, August 19, 2019, Document ID: 3c899e6e-c185-4fe9-b006-0f73c74b4c5a, http://www.ala.org/advocacy/diversity/librariesrespond/Services-LGBTQ; Committee on Professional Ethics (COPE), "Professional ethics," American Library Association, May 19, 2017, revised June 29, 2021, document ID: 39f580a8-833d-5ad4-f900-53ecfe67eb1f, http://www.ala.org/tools/ethics.

9. "Explore the shared foundations," National School Library Standards, n.d., https://standards.aasl.org/; American Association of School Librarians, "Shared foundations: Include," National School Library Standards, [November] 2017, https://standards.aasl.org/wp-content/uploads/2017/11/SharedFoundations_Include_2017.pdf.

10. American Association of School Librarians, "AASL cosponsors 'Jazz & Friends National Day of School and Community Readings' with HRC's Welcoming Schools and NEA," *Knowledge Quest, Journal of the American Association of School Librarians*, January 29, 2021, https://knowledgequest.aasl.org/aasl-cosponsors-jazz-friends-national-day-of-school-and-community-readings-with-hrcs-welcoming-schools-and-nea/.

11. See Appendix 3 for an example of this type of guidance around classroom material.

12. Liberal Jane Illustration, If Your Activism Isn't Accessible and Inclusive Who Is It Even For?, https://liberaljane.store/collections/digital-downloads/products/digital-download-products-if-your-activism-isnt-accessible-and-inclusive-who-is-it-even-for.

13. Liberal Jane Illustration, Inclusive Curriculums Benefit All Students, https://liberaljane.store/collections/digital-downloads/products/digital-download-inclusive-curriculums-benefit-all-students.

14. Available for free online: "Developing a gender inclusive school," HRC Foundation, n.d., https://welcomingschools.org/resources/framework-for-developing-a-gender-inclusive-school.

15. Ashlee Craft, quoted in Daylina Miller, "Trans joy: Living authentically inspires others to do the same," WUSF Public Media—WUSF 89.7, April 27, 2022, https://wusfnews.wusf.usf.edu/local-state/2022-04-26/trans-joy-living-authentically-to-inspire-others-to-do-the-same.

16. "Creating safe and welcoming schools," Human Rights Campaign Foundation, n.d., www.welcomingschools.org; "Fostering inclusive classrooms," Pride and less prejudice, n.d., www.prideandless prejudice.org.

17. "Maddy" is sometimes used by children with a trans parent as a combination of "mommy" and "daddy."

18. Learn about GLSEN's Rainbow Library and request books at www .rainbowlibrary.org.

19. Cris Mayo, *LGBTQ Youth and Education: Policies and Practices* (New York: Teachers College Press, 2014), 78.

20. Jennifer C. Smith-Grant, Nancy D. Brener, Adriana Rico, and J. Michael Underwood, "Profiles 2020: School Health Profiles Characteristics of Health Programs among Secondary Schools," Atlanta: Centers for Disease Control and Prevention, 2022, p. 1, https://www.cdc.gov/healthyyouth/data/profiles/pdf/2020/CDC-Profiles-2020.pdf.

21. "Profiles 2020," pp. 23, 26 (note 99), https://www.cdc.gov/healthyyouth/data/profiles/pdf/2020/CDC-Profiles-2020.pdf; Lilly Quiroz and Audrey Nguyen, "Sex education often leaves out queer people. Here's what to know," *NPR*, updated August 30, 2022, https://www.npr.org/2021/04/22/989826953/sex-ed-often-leaves-out-queer-people-heres-what-to-know.

22. "About advocates for youth," n.d., https://www.advocatesforyouth
.org/about/.

23. "Amaze Is Free and Always Will Be," Amaze, Advocates for Youth,
n.d., https://amaze.org/what-is-amaze/.

24. "Profiles 2020," p. 30, https://www.cdc.gov/healthyyouth/data/
profiles/pdf/2020/CDC-Profiles-2020.pdf.

25. "The SIECUS State Profiles 2019/2020," SIECUS (Sex Ed for Social
Change), n.d., https://siecus.org/state-profiles-2019-2020/.

26. "Chapter 4: Strategy 2C—Safe and Supportive Environments (SSE),"
Centers for Disease Control and Prevention, n.d., p. 76, https://
www.cdc.gov/healthyyouth/programguidance/pdf/PS18-
1807_guidance_chapter4.pdf.

27. Gabriel, A., Stratford, B, & Steed, H. (2021). Only 9 States and DC
Report That More Than Half of Secondary Schools Have a Gender
and Sexuality Alliance. Child Trends. https://www.childtrends.
org/blog/only-9-states-and-the-district-of- columbia-report-that-
more-than-half-of-secondary-schools-have-a-gender-and-sexuality-
alliance.

28. Jane G. Rainey, "Equal Access Act of 1984," The First Amendment
Encyclopedia, Free Speech Center at Middle Tennessee State
University, n.d., https://www.mtsu.edu/first-amendment/
article/1077/equal-access-act-of-1984; "Equal Access Act,"
K12academics.com, n.d., https://www.k12academics.com/
us-education-legislation/equal-access-act.

29. Andy, "The average height of NBA players from 1952–2022," The
Hoops Geek blog (citing data from basketballreference.com), last
updated July 4, 2022, https://www.thehoopsgeek.com/average-
nba-height/; Ishan Daftardar, "Scientific analysis of Michael
Phelps's body structure," Science ABC, last updated July 8, 2022,
https://www.scienceabc.com/sports/michael-phelps-height-arms-
torso-arm-span-feet-swimming.html.

30. Ruth Padawer, "The humiliating practice of sex-testing female athletes," *New York Times*, June 28, 2016, https://www.nytimes .com/2016/07/03/magazine/the-humiliating-practice-of-sex-testing-female-athletes.html; Lindsey Darvin, "Florida will no longer ask high school athletes about their menstrual cycles, but many states still do," WFXR Fox TV, updated February 26, 2023, https://www.wfxrtv.com/news/national-news/florida-will-no-longer-ask-high-school-athletes-about-their-menstrual-cycles-but-many-states-still-do/; "'They're chasing us away from sport': Human rights violations in sex testing of elite women athletes," Human Rights Watch, December 4, 2020, https://www .hrw.org/report/2020/12/04/theyre-chasing-us-away-sport/human-rights-violations-sex-testing-elite-women.

CHAPTER SEVEN

Disrupt

"Change doesn't happen if we just wait for others to do things. If I
want to see change happening, really, it has to have to come from me."
—Bob Chikos (he/him), teacher,
parent of a trans child

UNFORTUNATELY, EDUCATION communities sometimes include
people who are uncomfortable discussing trans identity, don't
prioritize supporting trans students, and may even be actively
seeking to harm trans people. Whether it's one individual student
making inappropriate jokes or picking on another student, a parent objecting to classroom discussions about LGBTQ identity, or
an elected official or other policymaker attempting to pass laws
or policies that harm trans students, there is always something
we can do to disrupt harm and attempt to steer things back
toward education, affirmation, and inclusion.

Ideally, school leaders and principals should be at the fore-
front of setting the tone—and be the main disrupter of anti-trans
sentiment. (It's worth noting that many teachers who leave their
school cite the principal, not the school as a whole, as why they're
leaving.[1]) As the face of the school, it's important that the person
in this role has plans in place to address pushback against trans
rights from other students, staff, and the broader community.

Whether you're a teacher, a principal, other support staff, or
a community member, we acknowledge that vocally supporting

trans and non-binary students—and disrupting those who would attack them—can be uncomfortable, particularly if it's new to you, and especially if your school or district isn't supportive of trans students. If that's the situation you're in, we encourage you to find allies in your community and return back to your core educational values. Ultimately, school should be a safe place for *all* students to learn, including those who are trans and non-binary.

Trans Joy

The suffering of transgender people is a policy choice disguised as an inevitability. This is why our joy—your joy—is so indispensable as a fuel for action. Particularly when the news of the world only seems to grow dimmer and darker, it's more critical than ever to prove transgender joy is a reality within our grasp. To prove that with the right material and social support, our lives can be as fulfilling and meaningful as anyone else's. That even when forces larger than us try to break our spirit, we can respond as forcefully and effectively with joy as we can with anger, defiance, and protest.

—Gillian Branstetter (she/her), Communications Strategist at the ACLU[2]

Responding to Students

Educators and staff set the tone in schools, and every staff member should make it clear that trans and non-binary students are supported. Similarly, students who bully, tease, harass, or otherwise mistreat trans students should be taken as seriously as any other harassment or bullying. Ideally, a school's nondiscrimination and anti-bullying policies will explicitly include trans and non-binary students as protected from discrimination and bullying. However, even if the policies do not explicitly protect trans students, we can always return to broader values of respect and inclusion; it's unlikely that any principal or administrator would object to a teacher requiring that students respect each other.

Crucially, educators should set the tone from day one, and maintain a consistent tone moving forward. For example, that means taking time to correct students who misgender someone, but it doesn't mean that the class needs to come to a halt. If a student seems to have made an honest mistake and used "she" instead of "they," the teacher may simply say, "*They*, not *she*," and move on. Educators should also take into account their students' existing levels of knowledge, and whether students simply need more learning and support around treating their trans and non-binary classmates with respect.

On the other hand, if it's clear that a student is intentionally mistreating a trans or non-binary student, it may be necessary to separate the students, have follow-up conversations with the student who is acting out, or consider other disciplinary options. Regardless of the specific approach you take, it's important to do *something* to address the situation and make clear to all students what behavior is and isn't considered acceptable.

Responding to Parents and Community Members

> "The three key characteristics of supportive principles are serving as a lead learner, employing a child-centered approach, and fostering strong school-family collaboration"
> —Melinda M. Mangin, *Transgender Students in Elementary School*[3]

Some parents or other community members may oppose the actions necessary to support trans and non-binary students. While it's important to be respectful and allow space for community input and feedback, those should not be used as an excuse to avoid supporting trans students. As educator Jessica Cisneros notes in Chapter 6: Include, that support should be non-negotiable.

Gender Spectrum, "a national organization committed to the health and well-being of gender-diverse children and teens through education and support for families, and training and guidance for educators, medical and mental health providers, and other professionals," has a number of useful resources for those interested in supporting trans and non-binary youth. With the organization's permission, we're including its Principles for Responding to Concerns here:

> When discussions take place about gender issues in school, they can be highly charged; the subject seems to raise a level of intensity for many that is unlike most other topics. The intensity can in turn create a negative feedback loop when the energy levels of both parties are highly charged. Since you cannot control what is happening for the other person, there are some steps you can take to minimize the potential conflict. The following strategies can serve to de-escalate highly charged situations:

1. **Slow things down.**

   a. Breathe.

   b. Soften your voice.

   c. Pause reflectively before responding to comments.

   d. If behind a desk, move out in front of it.

   e. Listen reflectively and rephrase what you've heard. "I think I heard you say that you are worried this work will confuse the children. Is that correct?"

2. **Appreciate the sharing of the question/concern:** Take a moment to set a positive, constructive tone by recognizing that this is being brought to your attention (even if it is the tenth conversation on the topic!).

   a. Thank you so much for caring enough about your school to discuss this with me.

   b. It sounds like you've really thought a lot about this.

   c. I can see this feels important to you.

3. **Try to learn what's underneath the question or concern:** In addition to rephrasing, ask probing questions to narrow down the issue that is most challenging for the person.

a. Can you say more about that?

b. Can you help me understand the impact this is having on you or your child?

c. What might we do to support your child, you, and your family?

4. **Bring your own experience/expertise to the table:** Fall back on the fact that you have a wealth of knowledge about schooling. Take confidence in the fact that you have navigated challenging situations previously.

a. Here is what I have observed over the years....

b. In similar situations in the past....

c. I can remember a time when a parent had a similar concern....

5. **Return to shared beliefs:** Identify common hopes for how school will be for all students.

a. Safety is something I think we can agree is important for every child here.

b. Kindness and respect are two values that we help every student learn and demonstrate.

c. Creating a more positive learning environment helps every child be more successful.

6. **School Mission and Values:** Invoke the commitments that have been made in writing about your school's larger purposes and approaches.

a. At our school, we believe that....

b. We think that one of the reasons parents want their children here is our commitment to....

7. **Confidentiality:** Remind them that you have a professional responsibility to protect the privacy of everyone at the school.

a. Just as I would never talk about your child or family with someone else, I would never talk about another child or family with you.

b. Invite a solution for their child (versus assuming the other child must change or adapt).

8. **Provide Resources:** Have information, such as short articles and websites, ready to share.

   a. Can I share some information that other parents have found helpful who had similar questions?

   b. I can see that you have many ideas about this subject. I will send you some links about this that I've found helpful to more fully understand these issues.

9. **Ask for Time:** There are moments when you may simply not have the time to provide a response that you feel good about. A question or point has been raised that you are not sure how best to respond.

   a. You've really given me a lot to consider here. I'd like to think more about our conversation, and check in with my colleagues. Perhaps we could set up a time to check back next week?

   b. I want to be able to give you and this subject the attention it deserves. Let's make an appointment to talk when we both can give this topic a bit more time and attention.

10. **Deepen your reserves of will and urgency:** Even with various approaches and language at the ready, difficult conversations can cause us to pause and even question our own commitment to gender inclusion. Keeping in mind some larger more universal themes can help steel educators to stand strong and remain firm in one's commitments. While steadfast in your beliefs about the importance of this work, in the moment others' confrontational stance can shaken one's resolve. By keeping in mind a few basic tenets about why this work matters and how it is being done, these challenging moments can be endured with your will to move forward fully intact

    a. Views about gender are evolving rapidly, especially among young people.

b. Work related to gender diversity benefits every student by creating safer environments in which to teach and learn.

c. Schools throughout the country are being very intentional about gender inclusion and successfully supporting transgender and non-binary students. While this may be new in your community, there are many, many places where this work has been happening for years.

d. Being uncomfortable is not the same as being unsafe.

e. Transgender and other gender-expansive students are at far greater risk than their cisgender peers.

f. In most cases, our kids are way ahead of the adults when it comes to this topic.[4]

It's important to remember that, while anti-trans voices may be the loudest, they often aren't in the majority. We spoke with four educators from a school district outside of Boston, Massachusetts. They worked together to implement a social and emotional learning (SEL) unit about transgender identities in 2021, and made sure to track community input and feedback:

> We actually kept track, the principals and myself had a table going of the responses. We wanted to make sure that we were able to articulate to anyone who asked—a school committee or anyone who asked—how many parents are upset. We also wanted to be able to say, "We received emails of support and encouragement for our work." One of the biggest things we've learned is, even if it feels like the negativity is constant and all around you, when we sat and looked at the numbers, it's not the majority of people. It was actually a smaller amount, even though it felt like a lot more.
>
> Some parents just want to have more information. They wanted their own learning. And so it opened an avenue to conversation. It was a continuum, an array of why people were reaching out.

FIGURE 7.1   AP Photo/Timothy D. Easley, Protesters of Kentucky Senate bill SB150 banning gender-affrming care for transgender youth, 2023.[5]

Responding to Anti-Trans Laws and Policies

As discussed elsewhere in this book, more and more states are introducing and passing laws and policies targeting transgender students. While a thorough examination of these laws could be a separate book, it's helpful to have a general understanding of what these laws look like and possible approaches for responding to them.

Curious about how educators are responding to these restrictions, we spoke with Michael Rady (he/him), the Senior Education Programs Manager at GLSEN, a "national network

What Do Anti-Trans Laws Look Like?

Most of the bills and policies attacking trans students fall into one of four categories:

1. Sports bans, which ban trans students from participating in athletics

2. Bathroom bans, which ban trans students from using the correct bathroom or locker room

3. Medical bans, which ban trans youth from accessing medically appropriate gender-affirming care

4. Censorship bills, including those which ban teachers from acknowledging trans people exist, those which ban teachers from using a student's chosen name and pronouns, or those which ban books (including anti-Black curriculum bills that ban teaching accurate and correct history)

It's important to note the harm these bills cause even when they *don't* pass, and even in states that don't have a single anti-trans bill introduced in the legislature: NPR found that—due to the recent increase of anti-trans policies and legislation—trans students across the country are worried about going to school; in cities and states that already have supportive policies and laws, trans students are worried about protections going away. Similarly, the Trevor Project found that the majority of LGBTQ youth are following the news about anti-trans legislation, and that it's harming their mental health.[6] For these reasons, Tim'm West (he/they), Executive Director of the National Center for Civil and Human Rights, calls what's happening now "legislative bullying":

> We're in a moment now that, as scary as it seems, the lines are pretty clear. And I think that the clarification of those lines, to ask, "Are you about providing equal support and equal education to *all* kids?" There's not room for "Well, we kind of do it sometimes."

(*Continued*)

(*Continued*)

It's a kind of legislative bullying. And [teachers] default to, "Well, I don't want to get in trouble, so I'm not going to talk about anything at all."

Some states and districts are also pushing policies that would explicitly require schools to out trans students to their parents or guardians. For example, in 2022, the Virginia Department of Education issued model policies and guidelines that contained the following language:

[School] personnel shall refer to a student by a name other than one in the student's official record, or by pronouns other than those appropriate to the sex appearing in the student's official record, only if an eligible student or a student's parent has instructed [School Division] in writing that such other name or other pronouns be used because of the student's persistent and sincere belief that the student's gender differs from his or her sex.[7]

While this model policy does not have the force of law, it sets a dangerous precedent for trans youth. Rodrigo Heng-Lehtinen (he/him), the Executive Director at the National Center for Transgender Equality, worried about the impact of this type of policy on trans youth, asking, "Who knows how those parents are going to react, who knows if they're going to be affirming or not, or even abusive and kick them [the trans youth] out in the worst-case scenario?" Heng-Lehtinen sees this type of policy "spreading like wildfire in the states and at the local level in schools," endangering students across the country.

Trans Joy

All the trans and non-binary kids will someday be voters who will vote for trans-affirming candidates, and that gives me hope.

—Griffin (she/her), 12

of educators, students, and local GLSEN chapters" working to ensure that students can access "a safe, supportive, and LGBTQ-inclusive K–12 education." GLSEN's Rainbow Library program provides free LGBTQ+ affirming K–12 text sets to schools in select states, and has a page on responding to anti-LGBTQ censorship attempts online at https://www.rainbowlibrary.org/censorship/. Rady explained:

> As these attacks have become broader, across more states, and better financed, we needed to rethink our approach. We need to be strategic and proactive in terms of the book selection process: incorporating book reviews from school library journals, book list.org, and others places, knowing many school systems have in their policies book review as part of their selection process. We're also making sure there are positive reviews for the books we're considering, to help make sure the books we're sending would already meet existing criteria and for the grade level.

The Trevor Project, an organization dedicated to "ending suicide among LGBTQ young people," is researching the impact of these anti-trans laws and policies across the country.[8] We spoke with Keygan Miller (they/them), Public Training Manager at The Trevor Project, about their work:

> *How has the current political landscape impacted your work?*
>
> There are states that are already more affirming to LGBTQ issues, and [those teachers are] like, "We must be more affirming, we must be super allies," which is great. But we're also seeing some folks who are afraid of asking for trainings and asking for resources, they're afraid of the backlash, particularly if they're not in positions of power. Teachers, for example, where they would love to be trained [on supporting LGBTQ students], but if they say "LGBTQ"

in any way shape or form in the classroom, are they going to then lose their career?

And, and that's not just in the states that are putting those bans forth. I had a trans teacher reach out to me the other day—in New Jersey, of all places—who was concerned about their job because of a parent who would log on to the school board and was complaining about their. . .basically their existence in the school. It doesn't matter how progressive places are, there's still more work to be done. And I think people are recognizing that.

How has the recent rise in anti-trans policies and legislation impacted trans students?

We're seeing an increase in mental health issues and suicidality across all young people, period, point blank. That in and of itself speaks volumes to our current culture and climate. And then, on top of that, we have LGBTQ young people who have experienced a different level of trauma during [the pandemic] of being in unsupportive homes and not having those outlets and those affirming spaces [in school] that they might be able to go to, a GSA or the like.

But we also see that the politics, the rhetoric, the lawmakers, talking about all these things is taking a toll on the mental health of LGBTQ people. 85% of trans and non-binary youth, and 66% of all LGBTQ youth, said that the debates around anti-trans laws negatively impacted their mental health. Those numbers speak for themselves, but I also want to point out that not 85% of our trans non-binary youth live in states where those bills were introduced. That means that they [trans youth] are not only being impacted

> when it's their state, but it's also when it's the next state over or when it's a state across the country that is just really loud.
>
> We have to consider that it's not just what happens at the end—we might not get it [an anti-trans policy or law], it might get vetoed, and that's great—but that rhetoric around it has already done the damage.

As you get to know your district and state laws (as well as those on the federal level, like Title IX, FERPA and The Equality Act), determining how you want to be an advocate educator is critical. It's also important to ask yourself what you would do if anti-trans laws or policies were passed in your state or your district. Will you be testifying at the state legislature? Wearing a pronoun pin? Calling trans and non-binary students by their preferred name and pronouns, even if the law says differently? There are many ways to support trans and non-binary youth, and to disrupt anti-trans rhetoric and action, regardless of the laws and policies where you live.

Trans Joy

Gender Euphoria is "a breath of fresh air" (transgender woman, 24), "trans celebration, happiness, wonder, hope," (non-binary, 21), "a moment of elation or connection with one's gender" (transmasculine non-binary, 25), "sheer joy and contentment," (non-binary/genderqueer, 34) and "a little shiny gender breakthrough" (non-binary, 24).[9]

Considering Legal Action

There may be times when what is happening in your school, district, or state is unlawful. Even if new anti-trans laws are enacted, there continue to be laws that teachers can lean on to ensure trans and non-binary students are safe. Ultimately, specific legal advice is outside the scope of this book, and neither of this book's authors are lawyers (even though one of us is the child of a lawyer and sometimes acts like she's one, too). Still, if you believe your school or district is proposing something illegal—for example, banning GSAs or implementing sex-segregated dress codes—you should speak up and object.

Fortunately, there are resources available online and organizations you can contact for support. You can start with local organizations and the state education agency or board of education, but you may also consider contacting the federal Department of Education or reaching out to national LGBTQ legal advocacy organizations like Lambda Legal or TLDEF (Transgender Legal Defense and Education Fund) or general advocacy organizations like PFLAG or the Trevor Project.

One of the most notable organizations regularly filing lawsuits in support of trans rights (what's referred to as "impact litigation") is the ACLU. In addition to extensive resources on students' rights, available online at https://www.aclu.org/know-your-rights/students-rights, the ACLU also has a specific helpdesk for those who have experienced mistreatment or harassment due to their sexual orientation, gender identity, or HIV status. Email helplgbtq@aclu.org with your name, pronouns, city and state, what happened, and what you hope the ACLU can do to help.[10]

Advocating *with* Trans Students and Student Voices

"Every year I got older, I just grew stronger. And I was like, nope, nope, nope! I really started having a voice and I was going to use it."
—Hayden Valentina Bisset (she/her), 16

Students are independent individuals whose wants and needs should be respected as much as possible. Likewise, as is discussed in Chapter 4: Educate, student voices can be a powerful, if not the most powerful, force in promoting change in education spaces. In Chapter 6: Include, we also learn that organizations like the National Council for the Social Studies (NCSS) have standards of practice that teach students to use their voice on issues they care about.

We spoke with Jim Bennett (he/him), Director of the Illinois Department of Public Health, about learning from and advocating with youth:

> I feel like I've learned so much [from youth]. I've learned to say what I think and what I feel, to value the self-exploration, and to not have answers right away.
>
> My godchild is trans, and I kept pushing to figure out, well, "What are the pronouns you're going to use? What's your name gonna be?" And they didn't need to make that decision right away, they were fine just figuring it out as they go. They weren't looking to immediately fit into a new box. That helped me a lot.
>
> I think that this generation coming up sees the country in a different way than I do. I grew up waiting for a correction when things went to the right. I just waited, like, "Oh, this is going to correct itself because we're not in the right place." And I don't think that this younger generation sees it in that way. They're more about their individual relationships, and not waiting on government to define what they can have or not have. Their expectation is they should be able to have everything that they know intuitively they deserve—that freedom feels right, that when they're free, and they're making their own choices, they're at peace. And it's an extraordinary gift that somehow this generation gets that we could all learn a lot from.

Sivan, a trans student, also provide us with advice for other students who want to be involved in advocacy:

> First of all, I would say, go for it. We need people who are willing to work to replace misinformation. And at the same time, do it in a safe way and think it through safely, whether that's speaking at your school and making sure that you have the administration support, in case there is any bullying afterwards or anything like that, or on a bigger level. For example, if you're going to speak to a company [about being trans], make sure that it's doing it for the right reasons. Make sure you have that support in case there are negative repercussions which, because of the world we live in, that's always a possibility. And make sure that you're doing it in the safest and best way possible.

Sivan's mom reinforced the idea that trans youth can and should speak out, and that there is support when doing so:

> There's actually a lot of support out there. You have to seek it out sometimes. Sivan 100% sought out and did a lot of work to be able to be [a public advocate]. That's very affirming in a lot of ways.
>
> Separate from that, Sivan got permission to actually use Instagram to kind of be out there. He also found other people, sought out other people who are these amazing trans advocates. He reached out to them, and then they talk to each other and support each other. They write back and forth to each other, they sometimes collaborate on ideas. That's been a huge boon for you and certainly for people who are in places where there's not the actual support around.
>
> I'm not a huge fan of social media, just as a mom and a human, but I think that this is actually going a long way. Even from sitting in your bedroom, you can

> find a lot of support that's out there for you. When
> people are in it together, they just automatically feel it
> together and feel like they have a relationship already,
> in the most beautiful, wonderful, supportive way.

You can also help students use publicly available resources to advocate for change. For example, the ACLU also has a series of letter templates that students can send to their school administration on topics ranging from addressing anti-LGBTQ bullying to censorship of LGBTQ students and ideas.[11] Chris Hampton (she/her), Youth and Program Strategist at the ACLU, explained:

> We have these open letters to schools on different
> topics for self-advocacy. They are on our letterhead
> with my boss's signature. They are "Dear Principal or
> Superintendent, You're being given this letter because
> you're not allowing students to start a GSA. . . ."
> They're on a bunch of different topics. We update
> them every couple of years. We also have a bunch of
> *frequent* frequently asked questions: an index about
> what we get asked a lot. So they're very similar to a
> demand letter that an ACLU lawyer would send. It's
> a letter that a student or parent can print out or email
> the link and give it to the school and say, "This is
> from the ACLU website, your school district's attorney
> should look at it."

Meanwhile, organizations like the OpEd Project (https://www.theopedproject.org/) have resources to help students write op-eds to submit to local newspapers. You may also want to check out the Youth Activism Project at https://www.youthactivismproject.org/, and the Southern Poverty Law Center's Learning for Justice resources at https://www.learningforjustice.org/topics/rights-activism.

Likewise, reflect on the needs you identify in your school or community: if students identify pronouns as an important issue to them, you can help them find or make pronoun pins or name tags. If they want to contribute to curriculum updates, you can find information on how your district or state creates and updates curriculum, and then support students in pushing for change. Even if there are legal or policy barriers that make it difficult for adults to offer direct support, you can still provide information on what laws and policies currently exist, and how students can work to change them. Educators can also teach students about their rights, for example, referencing *Tinker v. Des Moines* in a discussion of the Vietnam War to emphasize students' First Amendment rights.

But while student voices can be powerful forces for change, students should never be forced to share their experiences or perspectives. Likewise, there may be drawbacks for students who speak out publicly. As a teacher, you may have opportunities to help elevate your students' voices in ways that may not be safe for them to do—emotionally or, sadly, physically.

With school board meetings being the new hot button place for anti-trans policies to be questioned (along with book bans and critical race theory), it may take a brave youth advocate to speak at a school board meeting. Consider Gavin Grimm: in 2015, he stood among an angry crowd, in front of a school board in Virginia to demand the ability to use the boys' restroom. He was 15 years old, targeted and bullied at school, and yet took the stand. (His story was turned into a great children's book coauthored by Grimm and Kyle Lukoff called *If You're a Kid Like Gavin: The True Story of a Young Trans Activist* (Katherine Tegen Books, 2022.). As an advocate educator, we don't want any of our youth to experience the trauma that may be inflicted on trans students who speak out publicly. On the other hand, some students may choose to take that risk.

In addition to finding support from organizations like the ACLU, Grimm also recommends student advocates stay mindful of "how you interact with social media and how you behave in public. We can get high emotions with thihgs, and we can be passionate, but it ultimately may not serve us or the people we're trying to defend."

Trans Joy

You Can Breathe Now

For so long

I've written my anguish

Translated it from pain to prose

So many lines about

Live with it, misshapen angel

Pull out my lungs, my ribs collapse

but what if I'm tired of living with it?

What happens if I can turn my rejoicing into rhyme?

Maybe I can write about

Sewing my pronouns into my jacket like skin

Hanging a pink, white, and blue flag on my wall

My joy can be beautiful, too

My pain isn't all the world should get to see

I am allowed to write with a smile

Run my hand down my flat chest

I could get used to these scars

(Continued)

(Continued)

> Someday children won't have to feel this way
>
> Someday all they'll feel will be joy
>
> I can't wait to see what poems they'll write
>
> —Jay Schroeder (he/they), 14

Award-winning librarian Julie Stivers shared similar concerns about student safety when she spoke with us, asking, "Doesn't that say something to you that I'm worried about my student safety for them just talking about how much they love to read?"

What is Stivers's way of "disrupting"? She asked students, safely within her library, about the importance of books and their thoughts on how books shaped them. Then, instead of inviting students to appear at a public hearing where vitriolic anti-trans things might be said, Stivers spoke on behalf of her students. To follow is a partial transcript of Stivers' remarks; the full testimony is available online:

> As a librarian, I nurture my students' literacy, their interests, and their full selves, all of my students. If a parent comes to me with a question about a book, the first thing I say is thank you. Thank you for being interested in the literacy and the reading life of your students. So that's how I'll start for anyone listening: thank you.
>
> Because books matter, and they matter when they are accessible to those that need them. Literacy is nurtured through choice, through availability, and through inclusion.
>
> All students that walked through the doors of the school library deserve to see themselves on the shelves,

their lived experiences. Recent book challenges are not about content; they are about identity. They are about denying all of our beautiful students the ability to see themselves reflected in the books in their libraries and classrooms. These challenges target Black, Latinx, and queer stories. Not only does this harm the students whose identities are authentically and thoughtfully portrayed in this literature, it harms all students who do not get to learn and build empathy.

I'm here to share the most important voices that can't be left out of this conversation—and that's students. The voices of our students. I'm reading nine student comments tonight—not to supplant their amazing voices, but to amplify them. Listen to our students' brilliance, empathy, and expertise. These are thoughts from students from across our district in regards to books that affirm our students' lived experiences, that affirm real history, and that affirm who they are.

"That book you gave me, I think it literally saved my life. That author gets me. The books in this space have made me love reading again."

"It's magical when a book tells you that you are no longer alone. Why does anyone want to take that experience from someone?"

"It feels safe for me to see things like this in a book for the first time instead of real-life whispering."

"Is it normal to cry from happiness while reading?"

"I mean, people know that reading about something in a book doesn't mean we'll go and do it, right?"

"Do they realize I read about dragons, and I don't start breathing fire?"

"I feel seen."

"Here's what I don't understand: when has banning books ever been a good idea? When have we ever looked back and said yeah, that was a smart move? Never."

"I'm here because you helped me find this book, I'm still here, and I'm breathing."[12]

Stivers also talked about "soft censorship," when a librarian might be asked to move a book to a different section, or bury it in a pile of other books, or not order specific LGBTQ-themed books. To that, Stivers notes:

> I know you feel pressure, and it's okay to feel pressure.
> And it's okay to think about, but we can't act on it. I
> can feel, and then I can act on the pressure to faith-
> fully reflect our students and affirm who they are.
> That's it. We're going to feel under pressure, but the
> only pressure we can act on is faithfully representing
> our students and affirming who they are. Full stop.
> And that's the job we signed up for. Right?

Evaluating Your Comfort with Taking Risks

Ultimately, advocating for trans and non-binary students may come with some risk. There are certainly subtle ways you can show support for trans students—subtle rainbows or trans flags in classroom artwork, providing resources or learning material that links to external LGBTQ content but is not in and of itself LGBTQ content, calling a student by their last name if you're not allowed to call a student by their preferred name—but you may be faced with a difficult decision: Do I support trans and non-binary students, and risk getting in trouble or even breaking the law, or do I stay silent?

Even worse, you may be asked to implement policies or follow guidelines that would be explicitly harmful to trans and non-binary students, such as in 2022 when Texas Governor Greg Abbott ordered mandated reporters—including teachers—

to report families with transgender children to the state's Department of Family and Protective Services, or 2023 when (as this book is being written) the Florida state government is attempting to require school employees to call students by the pronouns that match the gender on their birth certificate, even if a parent or guardian the student has given permission to do otherwise.[13]

Of course, this isn't the first time that educators have been forced to pick between what is right and what is legal. Tim'm West, Executive Director of the LGBTQ Institute at the National Center for Civil and Human Rights, put it this way:

> We need to be really inventive and creative about ways to provide support outside of the system. We got to do things underground, we got to be scrappy, we got to be inventive and creative. I mention that in the context of African American tradition because we learned to read when it was illegal to read. It was risky, but we did it.
>
> So if we look at the tradition of marginalized groups of people, we never used "we don't have the laws on our side" as an excuse. I think it's a walk and chew gum thing. We have to work to change the legislation, but it doesn't mean we don't also do the work. We have to get together and be really inventive and creative about how, because for me supporting non binary and trans kids is non-negotiable; I'm going to do it.
>
> So if I have to find a way to do it under the radar—that's illegal, that lands me in jail because I affirmed a queer kid—I'm willing to take that risk. I know not everybody is, and I don't think it's wrong if people say they're not willing to take that risk. But I think that there are people willing to take that risk, just like there were people that were Freedom Riders who went down South to fight for civil rights.
>
> It's not to put the lack of Black civil rights and LGBTQ civil rights on the same plane, but there's a

common thread of bullying people into segregation in America. And there was a time when people said, "We're not going to be bullied. We're still going to do the work." There's the principle of being truly committed to civil and human rights for everybody.

Unfortunately, the current political and legal climate means that you may need to evaluate your own comfort for risk-taking and ask yourself:

- What are the pros and cons if I publicly speak out in support of trans and non-binary students?

- What existing school material can I lean on (e.g., school mission statement or values) as I push to support trans and non-binary students?

- What is my personal comfort level of being the center of attention in these conversations?

- What are the potential personal and professional ramifications if I. . .

  - Call trans and non-binary students by their preferred name and pronouns?

  - Privately disagree with anti-trans policies or laws?

  - Publicly disagree with anti-trans policies or laws?

  - Speak out at PTA meetings, school board meetings, city council meetings, or other public gatherings?

- What will my financial situation be if my job is threatened because I supported trans and non-binary students?

Taking Care of Yourself

Working to disrupt anti-trans sentiment can be exhausting. That's why it's especially important to find allies and avoid doing this work alone, without support. You can likely find amazing allies who already exist in your community. If not, take advantage of online communities and resources, and think about how you can build and grow allyship in your offline community.

Taking care of yourself may mean being brave enough to ask for help. We spoke with Lisa Forman (she/her), founder and executive director of Pride and Less Prejudice (PLP), and Becca Damante (she/her) the co-founder and outreach coordinator of PLP, an organization that provides "LGBTQ-inclusive books to Pre-K through 3rd grade classrooms to help students and teachers 'Read out loud, read out proud!'"

Since its inception in November 2019, PLP has raised more than $140,000 and sent more than 8,000 LGBTQ-inclusive books to all 50 U.S. states and across Canada. Becca explained, "It never hurts to ask. The worst someone can do is say no or ignore you. To get 13 LGBTQ+ celebrities in our campaign video, we reached out to at least 100 publicists."

It's also normal to feel drained by this work—you may hear terms like battle fatigue or compassion fatigue to describe people who have given it their all.

No one can do everything, but everyone can do something.

Putting It into Practice

Following are scenarios to consider about addressing real-world challenges and personal reflection questions to ask yourself. We encourage you to take some time to reflect and catch your breath before taking action.

Personal Reflection Questions

1. What is your comfort level around public speaking? If you don't want to speak publicly, how else could you disrupt?

2. What students, teachers, and parents do you know who would be good voices to elevate to effect policy (or practice) change at your school, district, or state?

3. How familiar are you with local and state LGBTQ or trans-specific organizations? What can you do to get more involved and/or find out how to support their work?

Addressing Real-World Challenges

1. Your students ask to start a GSA and want you to be the advisor! When you go and meet with the principal, she says that a GSA is not allowed. What do you do? How do you advocate for your students?

2. Your state has a legislative session this winter and there are numerous anti-trans bills on the docket. How could you uplift student and teacher voices to disrupt the narrative the opposition was putting out? What might you do to help advocate?

3. The local school board is hearing complaints about a newly published, award-winning book with a trans main character. What do you do?

4. Given your current role and situation, what real-world challenges does this section bring up for you in your community? How might you approach those challenges? What resources currently exist from your school/district/board of education to handle these challenges?

5. If your current role changed, how might your thoughts on these challenges change? Think about how you might answer differently as a classroom teacher, a school principal, a district administrator, and so on.

Notes

1. Teaching Policy Fellows, "Musical chairs: Teacher churn and its impact on Indianapolis Public Schools," Teach Plus, n.d., https://teachplus.org/wp-content/uploads/files/publication/pdf/musical_chairs.pdf.

2. Gillian Branstetter, "Trans joy is most necessary when it feels the most impossible," ACLU, June 17, 2022, https://www.aclu.org/news/lgbtq-rights/trans-joy-is-most-necessary-when-it-feels-the-most-impossible.

3. Melinda M. Mangin, *Transgender Students in Elementary School: Creating an Affirming and Inclusive School Culture* (Boston: Harvard Education Press, 2020), p. 65.

4. "Principles for responding to concerns," Gender Spectrum, n.d., https://genderspectrum.org/articles/responding-to-concerns-principles.

5. AP Photo/Timothy D. Easley, Protesters of Kentucky Senate bill SB150 banning gender-affrming care for transgender youth, 2023, https://newsroom.ap.org/editorial-photos-videos/detail?itemid=8766283f5ccc4352848130aca6a2b0fa.

6. Michaela Winberg, "Trans students say they are nervous to go to school under anti-trans legislation," All Things Considered, WHYY, NPR, September 8, 2022, https://www.npr.org/2022/09/08/1121869386/trans-students-say-they-are-nervous-to-go-to-school-under-anti-trans-legislation; "Issues impacting LGBTQ youth: Polling analysis," *Morning Consult*, The Trevor Project, January 2022, https://www.thetrevorproject.org/wp-content/uploads/2022/01/Trevor Project_Public1.pdf.

7. "2022 model policies on the privacy, dignity, and respect for all students and parents in Virginia's public schools," Virginia Department of Education, n.d., https://www.doe.virginia.gov/programs-services/student-services/student-assistance-programming/gender-diversity.

8. "Explore Trevor," The Trevor Project, n.d, https://www.thetrevorproject.org/explore/.

9. Will J. Beischel, Stéphanie E. M. Gauvin, and Sari M. van Anders, "'A little shiny gender breakthrough': Community understandings of gender euphoria," *International Journal of Transgender Health* 23, no. 3 (2022): 274–294, https://doi.org/10.1080/26895269.2021.1915223.

10. "Report LGBTQ/HIV Discrimination," ACLU, n.d., https://action.aclu.org/legal-intake/report-lgbtqhiv-discrimination.

11. "LGBTQ students: Letters for when you're fighting discrimination," ACLU, letters updated February 2023, https://www.aclu.org/lgbtq-students-letters-when-youre-fighting-discrimination.

12. Julia Stivers, "Wake County school librarian defends challenged LGBTQ books," February 4, 2022," YouTube video, 2:45, https://www.youtube.com/watch?v=2qJVCttLjng.

13. Casey Parks, "He came out as trans. Then Texas had him investigate parents of trans kids," *Washington Post*, September 23, 2022, https://www.washingtonpost.com/dc-md-va/2022/09/23/texas-transgender-child-abuse-investigations/; Ana Ceballos, "Student pronoun restrictions in Florida schools gets OK from Senate committee," *Tampa Bay Times*, last updated March 20, 2023, https://www.tampabay.com/news/florida-politics/2023/03/20/pronouns-transgender-lgbtq-schools-parents-desantis/.

Conclusion

WE LIVE in odd times. For some trans youth, there has never been a better time to be a student: there are legal protections and informed school staff and supportive parents and wonderful local trans communities. For some trans youth, there has never been a more difficult time to be a student: there are anti-trans laws and policies and ignorant school staff and unsupportive parents and little or no local trans community. But we're all in this together, and advocating for and with trans and non-binary students is key to ensure that the trans and non-binary students of today grow into the amazing adults of tomorrow.[1]

We spoke with Levi Arithson (he/they), Program Manager of LGBTQ+ Equity Initiatives at Denver Public Schools, about what's missing from conversations about supporting trans and non-binary students. He said:

> The first thing that is missing is queer joy. We really are relying on our damage-centered narratives, and we really miss out on the wholeness of our youth. I always say, "We don't need our youth to be on the brink of suicide to be proactive." It's not to say that the statistics [about trans youth] aren't bad or terrifying. But it's so much more than that.

—Felix Duarte (he/they), 15

Rachel Altobelli (she/her), Director of Library Services and Instructional Materials for Albuquerque Public Schools, agreed:

> There are just not enough everyday joyful, happy books [featuring trans main characters] where the point is not a coming out story, or coming to terms. But just doing things: Going on a quest, solving a mystery, not liking the substitute teacher.

With that in mind, we asked some trans youth what brings them joy and gives them hope for the future:

- "Freedom to explore my gender." —Zephyr (she/they), 8
- "My friends and family that support me!" —Josh (they/them), 8
- "Being myself. —Ellie (they/them), 11
- "It gives me hope that I can grow up the way I want to be and not the way other people wish for me to be." —Ian (they/them), 11

- "We are slowly making our way toward being more accepted in the larger community, more safe spaces are being created and hopefully in the future people won't be so judgmental and they will be more accepting and those safe spaces will not be needed." —Emma (she/her), 14

In every case, advocate educators will be key to making those hopes into reality.

In the Introduction, we asked you to consider five questions:

1. Why did you become an educator?

2. What do you believe about children and learning?

3. How have issues of gender and gender diversity shown up in your professional work?

4. What is your comfort level in discussing these issues with students? Colleagues? Parents and community members

5. What do you think it would mean for YOU to be an advocate educator?

Now is the time to move from thought to action. So we'll leave you with one final question:

As an Advocate Educator, what are you going to do now?

Note

1. In August, 2023, as this book was being prepared to go to print, HRC released its 2023 LGBTQ+ Youth Report, which emphasizes the wide range of experiences–both positive and negative–facing LGBTQ+ youth. The report can be found online at https://reports .hrc.org/2023-lgbtq-youth-report

Afterword—
Vanessa Ford

"When you are confronted with a problem, always ask yourself,
'What's best for kids?' No matter the barriers, fight for what's best."

THIS QUESTION, posed by my father, a career elementary school
principal, has guided my path as an educator and as a parent.
My father was the quintessential teacher and administrator—the
perfect mix of kind, thoughtful, and loving—and always, *always*
focused on what was best for kids.

I grew up in a small town in New Hampshire, surrounded
by nature . . . and little diversity of any kind. Early on, my parents knew they wanted us to have a better understanding of the
world, so we would rent out our house each summer and jump
in an old VW van with a pop top and travel the country for six
weeks. From late nights at truck stops, to our chosen family in
the deep South of Mississippi, I grew up knowing that the world
was a beautifully diverse place. I was challenged to understand
my own biases as a young girl and be open to experiences that
were far different from my own. Building empathy along the way,
I saw the ways that our country had historically marginalized so
many people—especially those who were Black or Brown—who
didn't fit the societal norms that white supremacy had built.

Fast forward to my first year teaching in DC Public Schools.
I entered my open-space classroom—no walls between classes,
with a broken window and no toilet paper in the restrooms—and

immediately knew I needed to fight for what's best for kids, and this situation wasn't what they needed. For the next 14 years, I taught in DC Public and Public Charter Schools, fighting for equity, access, and opportunity for all of my students, particularly those who were at risk of missing out on meaningful, safe, learning environments.

Little did I know that as I had my own children, I would have to navigate the system also asking "What's best for kids?" and have those kids be my own. Ultimately, all parents have to advocate for their kids, and all teachers have to advocate for their students. As parents or educators or simply adult allies, we all think about how to answer that question: What's best for kids?

My world was challenged when, on my younger child's fourth birthday, they told us, "I'm not a boy. I'm a girl in my heart and in my brain." What was best for *my* kid in this situation? What was best for my child who then started to draw themselves as a girl, asked to be called sister, and wanted to wear more "feminine" clothing? We didn't know what the answer was, but we did know we had to listen.

When my family decided to enter the advocacy realm we had a lot to consider. Was it safe for us to do so? What value would telling our story have to others? How could our story inform what others would do in their lives? Did we have a story that would benefit others and lead to more understanding for transgender people? Most importantly, how would our child feel about sharing their story—at the time and in the future? To the final question, we decided that while our trans child couldn't give their consent due to their age, we would share details and information about what we did with them as parents, and the why, regularly checking in with our child and offering to stop at any time they wanted us to. We also knew that we would not do anything that we viewed as sensationalized or exploitative of trans identities and that we would only participate if we could answer yes to the question "Will our child look back and see the purpose behind what we did and be proud of it?" All of this to say, we didn't enter into advocacy lightly, or alone.

What quickly became clear was the extensive work still needed for a school to be prepared to welcome and support transgender students. It took a lot of research, talking to other families, learning the laws, and building relationships with the school staff to ensure that our child could enter Pre-K as their true self.

Then, the 2016 presidential election occurred. The conversation about trans youth turned toxic, and the toxicity has only increased since then. But, in response, amazing advocates were speaking out: I connected with Gavin Grimm, Bex Mui, my co-author Rebecca Kling, and many of the other wonderful advocates and activists quoted throughout this book. Our lives grew exponentially richer even during this immensely difficult time.

As we became more outspoken as advocates for trans rights, my husband and I started working on our children's book, *Calvin*. While inspired by our trans child, the book is intentionally not a retelling of their story. In particular, we wanted to write a book that had a transgender boy as the main character; at the time, most literature had gender creative boys or transgender girls, but representation was missing for trans boys. We wanted to show what was possible in a child's transition—that it can be done without pushback or bullying. Finally, we wanted to ensure representation of Black and Brown main characters, to celebrate our two beautiful biracial children. *Calvin* was published in late 2021, and we have been blown away by the positive response it has received.

Since I first started speaking publicly on trans rights, I have had parents and teachers contact me on a weekly basis, asking, "How can I best support transgender and non-binary students in our school community?" This book—the one you're reading right now—is the answer to that question, but it's not the *only* answer. This book is an amalgamation of experiences, resources, and best practices formatted into buckets that are easy to understand, and I hope you'll find it useful. But I also would love to hear your thoughts and learn from the work you're doing!

I look forward to fighting for trans and non-binary students alongside you,

—Vanessa Ford

Afterword—
Rebecca Kling

LIKE MANY millennials, my first exposure to transgender identity was on daytime talk shows: Ricki Lake, Sally Jessy Raphael, and (of course) Jerry Springer. The trans people I saw on those shows were almost always trans women described as "hiding" what they really were, accused of "tricking" the people in their life, often with a dramatic reveal to a boyfriend, husband, or family member who would inevitably react with anger, and sometimes with violence. These talk shows—along with movies like *Ace Ventura* (parodying *The Crying Game*) or police procedurals (with dead trans sex workers)—taught me that, while trans people existed, we were (at best) the butts of jokes and (at worst) the victims of deadly violence.

I also learned about trans identity online, using a 1990s dial-up Internet connection to explore chat rooms on America Online and visit personalized GeoCities pages with flashing backgrounds and tinny electronic music playing through my small desktop speakers. While the Internet allowed me to connect with and learn from actual trans people, the lessons were similar to those I gained from talk shows: being trans was (at best) incredibly difficult and (at worst) would result in losing your job, your spouse, your home, your life. Trans people could be laughed at, we could be sexualized, we could be victimized, we could be brutalized—but we could never be happy.

Fortunately, my lived experience as a trans woman has not lived up (or lived down?) to those awful expectations. I've had a mix of incredible luck and incredible privilege, and most of the things I was told to fear never came to pass. My parents didn't kick me out. I didn't end up poor and destitute. My friends and family didn't abandon me. I was, for the most part, accepted when I came out as trans. But there's an important distinction between "acceptance," a passive act, and "support," which requires action. The people in my life were overwhelmingly accepting, but they didn't know how to be actively supportive.

When I came out to my parents at 14, I said, "I think I want to be a girl." That was the language that made sense to me at the time; identifying as trans was too scary.

My mom quickly replied, "We will always love you."

My dad echoed her sentiment, "We will love you no matter what. As long as you're not a Republican." (My dad is still proud of this joke.)

This passive acceptance—this love—was crucial. But my parents didn't know how to be actively supportive. In the late '90s, there were no books about supporting trans children, no shows with authentic trans characters written by actual trans writers and played by actual trans actors, no gender clinics at major hospitals. The Gay Straight Alliance at my high school didn't have any resources for trans students and (as far as I know) there were no out trans teachers or classmates at school. Similarly, the local LGBT youth group I attended (they hadn't added a Q to their name yet) had resources and knowledge about how to support LGB youth, and not much to offer a closeted trans teen.

Things have undoubtedly changed since the '90s. Today there are conferences for trans youth, trans adults, families, educators, medical providers, and more. There are books for every age range—from short picture books to impressive works of literature—by trans authors and featuring trans characters. Transgender identity is mentioned in textbooks and talked about in college courses. It's now possible to find trans actors playing trans roles on television and film and on stage, and some of those roles were even written by trans writers. There are transgender superheroes and video game characters. There are trans elected officials holding public office. And critically, in many parts of the United States, discriminating against trans people is explicitly illegal, and courts consistently find that anti-trans discrimination is a type of sex discrimination, even in places where those explicit trans protections don't exist.

I've been lucky enough to see some of those positive changes firsthand. For more than a decade, I've worked with Harbor Camps (previously called Camp Aranu'tiq), a camp for trans and gender variant youth. Camp has grown from its first summer of about 30 campers staying for a single weeklong session to almost 500 campers per summer, across multiple sessions. I've gone from being a bunk counselor to a member of the leadership team, working with fabulous transgender peers and cisgender allies to provide a classic summer camp experience—complete with arts and crafts, s'mores at the campfire, a raucous variety show, canoeing, kickball, archery, and so much more—to transgender and gender-variant children ages 8 to 15.

In the last few years, we've even had former campers return as counselors-in-training, meaning Harbor Camps is one of the few places where trans adults (leadership and counselors) are working with trans young adults (counselors-in-training) to support trans youth (campers). Informal networks have always existed, where more knowledgeable members of the trans community support people who are newly out, but thinking about what we've established at Harbor Camps—an intergenerational passing of knowledge and skills and experiences between generations of transgender people—gives me chills; it would have been unimaginable just a few short years ago.

Of course, the last few years has also seen an intense and malignant push back against trans rights.

For all the difficulties of trans advocacy, this is where I was fortunate enough to meet my co-author, Vanessa Ford, and her family. Vanessa and I became fast friends, and immediately connected over our experiences as educators and our desire to see trans children protected, supported, and uplifted. We both firmly believe that getting to know trans people is the best way to turn skeptics into allies, but also that explicit policies are critical to protect transgender people from both intentional discrimination and unintentional ignorance.

Those shared beliefs are a large part of why we wrote this book together. The individual pieces are from a wide variety of sources—our own lived experiences, our backgrounds as educators, model policies from school districts and nonprofits, the collected wisdom of everyone we interviewed for this book—but the actual framework is all Vanessa. From her time as a classroom teacher, she realized those tools can be helpfully slotted into the four categories that structure this book: *Educate* teachers and staff about trans identity and supporting trans students; *Affirm* the identity and experience of trans youth; *Include* trans and gender variant representation in curriculum and school communication; and *Disrupt* individuals or systems that might work to (intentionally or unintentionally) harm trans students.

We don't pretend that this is the only way to think about supporting transgender students. Still, we're deeply proud of what this book provides and hope you find its tools a useful addition to your toolbox.

Whether you are a classroom teacher, a school administrator, a parent or guardian of a trans child, or simply someone wanting to learn more about supporting trans students, thank you for taking the time to learn and grow. If you're a transgender person—a student or an adult, a professional advocate or a curious community member—we hope you'll find these tools useful as well.

No one can do everything, but everyone can do something. And together, we can build classrooms, schools, school districts, and an entire society where trans youth can thrive.

Stay strong, and stay in touch.

—Rebecca Kling

Acknowledgments

THE ADVOCATE *Educator's Handbook* only came to fruition through the support of many incredible people.

As we began to plan *The Advocate Educator's Handbook*, we knew that we wanted to elevate the voices of experts, professionals, trans adults and youth, legislators, and organizers who lead the work every day in their communities. Thank you to nearly 60 individuals, organizations, and members of the community we interviewed. Specifically, thank you to Alisa Kotler-Berkowitz, Armonte Butler, Bex Mui, Bob Chikos, Booker Marshall, Brittni Lara, Cheryl Greene, Chris Hampton, Danica Roem, Daniel Trujillo, Dave Edwards, Dr. David Johns, E. O., Finn Gratton, Gabrielle Montevecchi, Gavin Grimm, Hannah Edwards, Dr. Harper Keenan, Hayden Valentina Biset, Heather Biset, Jim Bennett, Jose Trujillo, Julie Stivers, Dr. Kathleen Either, Keygan Miller, Kristen Hamilton, Dr. Kristina Olson, Kyle Lukoff, Levi Arithson, Lisa Foreman, Lisa Keating, Lizette Trujillo, Logan Casey, Dr. Melinda Mangin, Nikki Neuen, R. G., Rachel Altobelli, Rae Jones, Rebecca Cokley, Becca Damante, Rodrigo Heng-Lehtinen, Dr. Russ Toomey, Sam Long, Sara Staley, Sarah McBride, Sivan Kotler-Berkowitz, Stella Keating, Tamara Jazwinski, Terrance "TJ" Johnson, Tim'm West, and Wesley Hedgepeth.

Thank you as well to Human Right Campaign's Welcoming Schools, the ACLU, Gender Spectrum, the Centers for Disease Control and Prevention, Advocates for Youth, A Queer Endeavor, the Trans Educator Network, the Trevor Project, GLSEN, the National Center for Civil and Human Rights, Danvers Public Schools, Beverly Public Schools, Denver Public Schools, Chicago Public Schools, the Ford Foundation, the National Black Justice Coalition, the YES! Institute, the National Center for Transgender Equality, the Human Rights Campaign, Gender Inclusive Schools, OutFront Minnesota, Pride and Less Prejudice, and Child Trends.

Your work is inspiring and, because of it, we are hopeful for the future.

Thank you to Sophie LaBelle for allowing us to use her comics (even though they didn't make it to the final draft), to Felix Duarte, Liberal Jane Illustrations, Andy Passchier, and art twink for the use of their art, Ginny Suss for the use of her photograph, and to Jay Schroeder and Keath Silva for the use of their poems.

Thank you to our Jossey-Bass editors, who trusted us to bring the first book about supporting LGBTQ youth to market for Jossey-Bass, and to our agents at Aevitas Creative, Rick Richter and Maggie Cooper, for guiding us throughout. Thank you to our developmental editor, Kirsten Janene-Nelson, for her diligent and eagle-eyed deep dive into the manuscript and her collaboration to bring this into its final form.

Thank you to our parents—our original educators, and some of our initial readers—for your questions and comments as we aimed to make this text accessible to all.

Thank you to our most loved partners who supported us throughout and our friends who cheered us along the way.

Thank you to Dr. Peggy Brookins for using her powerful voice and expertise to support this work.

We thank each other—best friends turned co-authors! Through over a year of intense work, we found a way to deepen our friendship, our commitment to the work and to transgender youth.

We thank you, the reader, for dedicating yourself to becoming an #AdvocateEducator, ensuring that all transgender and non-binary youth in your communities have you to turn to. Please share this book with your friends, colleagues, and the world. Form book groups, discuss content and use social media to spread your learning (#AdvocateEducator) to ensure that all transgender youth have trusted adults to support their excellence.

Finally, we thank trans and non-binary youth everywhere. You are our inspiration, our passion, and our guides. You belong everywhere and we know you will change the world for the better. We love you and will forever be by your side.

—Vanessa and Rebecca

Appendix 1: Additional Resources

Books

Dude, You're a Fag: Masculinity and Sexuality in High School, with a New Preface by C. J. Pascoe (University of California Press, 2011).

The Educator's Guide to LGBT+ Inclusion by Kryss Shane (Jessica Kingsley Publishers, 2020). (https://us.jkp.com)

The Gender Creative Child: Pathways for Nurturing and Supporting Children Who Live Outside Gender Boxes by Diane Ehrensaft (The Experiment, 2016).

Histories of the Transgender Child by Julian Gill-Peterson (University of Minnesota Press, 2018). "Recommended Books for Adults" by HRC and Welcoming Schools. (https://hrc-prod-requests.s3-us-west-2.amazonaws.com/welcoming-schools/documents/WS-Recommended-Books-for-Adults.pdf)

Safe Is Not Enough: Better Schools for LGBTQ Students by Michael Sadowski (Youth Development and Education Series, Harvard Education Press, 2016).

Shared Foundations Series Bundle by American Association of School Librarians (AASL) (2019–Fall 2023). (https://www.alastore.ala.org/content/shared-foundations-series-bundle)

Spectrums: Autistic Transgender People in Their Own Words edited by Maxfield Sparrow (Jessica Kingsley Publishers, 2020). (https://us.jkp.com)

Supporting Transgender Autistic Youth and Adults: A Guide for Professionals and Families by Finn V. Gratton (Jessica Kingsley Publishers, 2019. (https://us.jkp.com)

Supporting Transgender Students: Understanding Gender Identity and Reshaping School Culture by Alex Myers (University of New Orleans Press, 2021).

The Teaching Transgender Toolkit by Eli R. Green and Luca Maurer (2015). (Teachingtransgender.org)

Transgender Students in Elementary School: Creating an Affirming and Inclusive School Culture by Melinda M. Mangin (Youth Development and Education Series, Harvard Education Press, 2020).

When the Drama Club Is Not Enough: Lessons from the Safe Schools Program for Gay and Lesbian Students by Jeff Perrotti and Kim Westheimer (Beacon, 2002).

Videos and Documentaries

The Biology of Gender, From DNA to the Brain, Karissa Sanbonmatsu, TED Women 2018. (https://www.ted.com/talks/karissa_sanbonmatsu_the_biology_of_gender_from_dna_to_the_brain?rid=txfZXRicTFUU)

Gender Revolution: A Journey with Katie Couric—A National Geographic special from 2016. (https://www.nationalgeographic.org/education/gender-revolution/)

It's Elementary: Talking about Gay Issues in School (1999) and *It's STILL Elementary*, both part of the Respect for All Project; plus additional films from GroundSpark. (https://groundspark.org/films)

Scholarly Articles, Research, and Data

Educating Educators: Knowledge, Beliefs, and Practice of Teacher Educators on LGBTQ Issues (GLSEN, Sept 2022). (https://www.glsen.org/sites/default/files/2022-09/GLSEN_Educating_Educators_092022.pdf)

"Examining the Relationship Between LGBTQ-Supportive School Health Policies and Practices and Psychosocial Health Outcomes of Lesbian, Gay, Bisexual, and Heterosexual Students," by Wojciech Kaczkowski, Jingjing Li, Adina C. Cooper, and Leah Robin *LGBT Health*, vol. 9, no. 1 (January 2022): 43–53. (https://doi.org/10.1089/lgbt.2021.0133)

"Gen Z GSAs: Trans-Affirming and Racially Inclusive Gender-Sexuality Alliances in Secondary Schools" by Madelaine Adelman, Sean Nonnenmacher, Bailey Borman, and Joseph G. Kosciw, *Teachers College Record: The Voice of Scholarship in Education* 124, no. 8 (September 2022): 192–219. (https://doi.org/10.1177/01614681221123129)

GLSEN: *The 2021 National School Climate Survey: The Experiences of Lesbian, Gay, Bisexual, Transgender, and Queer Youth in Our Nation's Schools* by Joseph G. Kosciw, Caitlin M. Clark, and Leesh Menard. (https://www.glsen.org/sites/default/files/2022-10/NSCS-2021-Full-Report.pdf)

"GSA Advocacy Predicts Reduced Depression Disparities Between LGBQ+ and Heterosexual Youth in Schools," by V. Paul Poteat, Hirokazu Yoshikawa, Sarah B. Rosenbach, S. Henry Sherwood, Emily K. Finch, and Jerel P. Calzo, *Journal of Clinical Child & Adolescent Psychology*, 2023. (https://doi.org/10.1080/15374416.2023.2169924)

"New Poll Illustrates the Impacts of Social & Political Issues on LGBTQ Youth" by Josh Weaver, The Trevor Project, January 10, 2022. (https://www.thetrevorproject.org/blog/new-poll-illustrates-the-impacts-of-social-political-issues-on-lgbtq-youth/)

"Research Shows Lack of Support for Transgender and Gender-Nonconforming Youth in U.S. School Systems" by Tonei Glavinic, *Inquiries Journal*, vol. 2, no. 1 (2010). (http://www.inquiriesjournal.com/articles/135/research-shows-lack-of-support-for-transgender-and-gender-nonconforming-youth-in-us-school-systems)

Sexual Orientation, Gender Identity, and Schooling: The Nexus of Research, Practice, and Policy edited by Stephen T. Russell and Stacey S. Horn (Oxford University Press, September 2016).

"Similarity in transgender and cisgender children's gender development" by Selin Gülgöz, Jessica J Glazier, et al., *Proceedings of the National Academy of Sciences of the United States of America*, vol. 116, no. 49 (2019). (https://doi.org/10.1073/pnas.1909367116)

"Support Saves Lives: Exploring the Relationship Between Age of Transition, Family Support, and Retrospective K–12 Educational Experiences in Transgender Suicidality" by Gabe H. Miller, Guadalupe Marquez-Velarde, Mario I. Suárez, and Christy Glass, *Transgender Health*, January 9, 2023. (https://doi.org/10.1089/trgh.2022.0073)

"The California Reducing Disparities Project," Gender Spectrum. (https://genderspectrum.org/articles/cdep-evaluation-project)

The Trevor Project: *2022 National Survey on LGBTQ Youth Mental Health.* (https://www.thetrevorproject.org/survey-2022/)

"Using a Queer of Color Critique to Work toward a Black LGBTQ+ Inclusive K–12 Curriculum" by Shamari Reid, *Curriculum Inquiry*, vol. 53, no. 2 (2023). (https://doi.org/10.1080/03626784.2022.2121594)

"'We Have No "Visibly" Trans Students in Our School': Educators' Perspectives on Transgender-Affirmative Policies in Schools" by Wayne Martino, Kenan Omercajic, and Jenny Kassen, *Teachers College Record*, vol. 124, no. 8 (2022): 66–97. (https://doi.org/10.1177/01614681221121522)

Welcoming Schools 2021 Annual Report, Human Rights Campaign Foundation. (https://reports.hrc.org/welcoming-schools-2021-annual-report)

Resources Intended Specifically for Educators

"An Age-by-Age Guide to Talking to Your Kids about Gender" by S. Bear Bergman, *Today's Parent*, October 17, 2022. (https://www.todaysparent.com/family/parenting/how-to-talk-to-kids-about-gender-age-by-age-guide/)

Anti-Bias Building Blocks: K–5 Curriculum from ADL (Anti-Defamation League), 2018. (https://www.adl.org/resources/tools-and-strategies/anti-bias-building-blocks)

Colorado Trans/Nonbinary Educators Network (CO-TEN). (https://www.facebook.com/TransEducators/)

Five Best Practices to Support and Learn from Trans Educators by Sam Long and Mckenzee Griffler, October 2019. (https://www.youtube.com/watch?v=4ReKjg-XUPM)

Five Core Propositions, National Board for Professional Teaching Standards: NBPTS. (https://www.nbpts.org/certification/five-core-propostions/)

Gender Triangle Education Guide. (https://www.glsen.org/sites/default/files/2019-11/GLSEN-Gender-Triangle-Education-Guide.pdf)

GLSEN's Solidarity Week is a "student-led program where LGBTQ+ students and educators in K–12 schools lead the conversation on how non-LGBTQ+ people can be in solidarity with them and also how they can show solidarity with others in their community." (https://www.glsen.org/programs/solidarity-week)

Illinois Safe School Alliance. (https://www.ilsafeschools.org/)

Open Letter to Schools about Gender and Sexuality Alliances and Gay-Straight Alliances, ACLU. (https://www.aclu.org/letter/open-letter-schools-about-gender-and-sexuality-alliances-and-gay-straight-alliances?redirect=letter/open-letter-schools-about-gay-straight-alliances)

A Queer Endeavor, University of Colorado Boulder. (https://www.colorado.edu/center/a-queer-endeavor/educator-resources)

Responding to Anti-LGBTQ Censorship Attempts, GLSEN Rainbow Library. (https://www.rainbowlibrary.org/censorship/)

Responsive Classroom is a "student-centered, social and emotional learning approach to teaching and discipline." (https://www.responsive classroom.org/)

Stonewall National Education Project (SNEP). (https://stonewall-museum.org/snep/snepsymposium/)

Supportive Schools for LGBTQ+ Students: A Guide to Policies and Best Practices, Campaign for Southern Equality. (https://southern equality.org/supportiveschoolsguide-2022/)

Talking to Young Children About Gender, Gender Spectrum. (https://genderspectrum.org/articles/talking-to-young-children)

Trans Educators Network. (https://www.transeducators.com/)

Sample Curriculum Resources

"The Framework: 5 Principles for Gender-Inclusion" developed by Sam Long. (https://www.genderinclusivebiology.com/framework-for-thihnking)

Gender-Inclusive Biology. "To support all students, present & future, we must adapt existing biology teaching to grow a gender-inclusive curriculum" (including lesson materials, guides, and more). (https://www.genderinclusivebiology.com/)

GLSEN: Advocate for Inclusive & Affirming Curriculum. (https://www.glsen.org/inclusive-curriculum)

Healthy Teen Network Tip Sheet: Gender, Sexuality, & Inclusive Sex Education. (https://www.healthyteennetwork.org/wp-content/uploads/Gender-Sexuality-Inclusive-Sex-Ed.pdf)

History UnErased: Intersections & Connections Curriculum. (https://unerased.org/)

LGBTQ+ Inclusive Curricula: School Curricula Inclusive of LGBTQ+ History, Culture, and People; Sex Education from the American Psychological Association. (https://www.apa.org/topics/lgbtq/lgbtq-inclusive-curricula)

Queer America: Incorporating LGBTQ History into Your Classroom w/ Daniel Hurewitz, Learning for Justice. (https://www.learning-forjustice.org/podcasts/queer-america/incorporating-lgbtq-history-in-your-classroom)

Welcoming Schools Lesson Resources. (https://welcomingschools.org/resources/lessons)

Wit & Wisdom is a "comprehensive K–8 English language arts curriculum crafted to help students build the knowledge and skills they need to be successful readers, exceptional writers, and effective communicators." (https://greatminds.org/english/witwisdom)

Courses and Professional Development for Educators

Decolonizing Gender by Bex Mui. (https://www.antiracisted.org/decolonizing-gender)

Supporting Transgender, Non-binary, and Gender Non-conforming Students. (https://www.nea.org/professional-excellence/professional-learning/resources/supporting-transgender-non-binary-and)

Trans Freedom Summer School: Recordings of "SOGI UBC and the University of Arizona's Trans Studies program are collaborating this summer to host a 3-part Trans freedom political education webinar series for youth, educators, and allies." (https://sogi.educ.ubc.ca/tfss/)

The Transgender Training Institute (TTI): Including Trans Topics across K–12 Curriculum, Supporting Transgender Students Coming Out, Gender Inclusive K–5 Classrooms. (https://www.eventbrite.com/cc/k-12-educators-47179)

Model Policies, Assessments, and Guidelines for Schools and Districts

Gender Inclusiveness Assessment: Framework for Gender Inclusive Schools, Gender Spectrum. (https://www.isbe.net/Documents/Gender-Inclusive-Assessment-Tool.pdf)

LGBTQ Inclusive School Assessment: GLSEN Professional Development Resources. (https://www.glsen.org/activity/LGBTQ-inclusive-school-assessment)

Model School District Policy on Transgender and Gender Non-conforming Students, GLSEN and NCTE, September 2018. (https://transequality.org/sites/default/files/images/resources/trans_school_district_model_policy_FINAL.pdf)

Real Policies and Guidelines for Schools and Districts

Anti-Racism Policy: Tacoma Public Schools. (https://resources.finalsite.net/images/v1655913787/tacomak12waus/kiqskfflojwhfvgipu7j/Policy1600_DRAFT_.pdf)

Gender Support Plan: Lake Forest Academy (IL). (https://www.lfanet.org/about-us/pluralism-and-multicultural-affairs/gender-support-plan)

Health and Family Life/Sex Education (Policy IHAM): Denver Public Schools. (https://go.boarddocs.com/co/dpsk12/Board.nsf/goto?open&id=C9CSJ472186B)

- LGBTQ+ Toolkit (Google Docs). (https://docs.google.com/document/d/1Jx_cvGAFsdYUP6FgTMZKeCFSjnx4Ic_01nlV7a19kL4/edit)

- LGBTQ+ Efforts—Denver Public Schools (DPS): Includes resources for schools and teachers, families, students, and more. (http://thecommons.dpsk12.org/site/default.aspx?pageid=2597)

Guidelines for Sexual Orientation and Gender Identity Inclusive Education: Los Angeles Unified School District, May 2014. (https:// achieve.lausd.net/cms/lib/CA01000043/Centricity/Domain/383/ BUL-6285.0.pdf)

Non-Discrimination and Equity: Tacoma Public Schools. (https:// www.tacomaschools.org/about/school-board/policy-manual/ policy-details-page/~board/policy-3000/post/3111)

Supporting Gender Diversity Toolkit: Chicago Public Schools. (https:// www.cps.edu/globalassets/cps-pages/services-and-supports/ health-and-wellness/healthy-cps/healthy-environment/lgbtq-supportive-environments/supportinggenderdiversitytoolkit2.pdf)

Professional Association Policy Positions and Best Practices

"Advocating for Transgender and Nonbinary Youths," 2022. (https://www .apa.org/monitor/2022/07/advocating-transgender-nonbinary-youths)

American Academy of Pediatrics: "Why We Stand Up for Transgender Children and Teens." (https://www.aap.org/en/news-room/aap-voices/why-we-stand-up-for-transgender-children-and-teens/)

American Library Association (ALA): Libraries Respond: Protecting and Supporting Transgender Staff and Patrons. (https://www.ala.org/ advocacy/diversity/librariesrespond/transgender-staff-patrons)

American Psychological Association (APA): "Guidelines for Psychological Practice with Transgender and Gender Nonconforming People," 2015. (https://www.apa.org/practice/guidelines/transgender.pdf)

American School Counselor Association: The School Counselor and Transgender and Nonbinary Youth. (https://www.schoolcounselor.org/ Standards-Positions/Position-Statements/ASCA-Position-Statements/ The-School-Counselor-and-Transgender-Gender-noncon)

HRC Foundation, NEA and American Association of School Librarians Sponsor Readings in Support of Transgender and Non-Binary Youth: Jazz and Friends National Day of School and Community Readings. (https://www.hrc.org/press-releases/hrc-foundation-nea-and-american-association-of-school-librarians-sponsor-readings-in-support-of-transgender-and-non-binary-youth)

National Association of School Psychologists (NASP): Transgender Youth. (https://www.nasponline.org/resources-and-publications/resources-and-podcasts/diversity-and-social-justice/lgbtq-youth/transgender-youth)

National Association of Secondary School Principals on supporting trans students. (https://www.nasponline.org/resources-and-publications/resources-and-podcasts/diversity-and-social-justice/lgbtq-youth/transgender-youth)

National Education Association (NEA): Legal Guidance on Transgender Students' Rights. (https://www.nea.org/resource-library/legal-guidance-transgender-students-rights); NEA LGBTQ+ Resources (https://www.nea.org/resource-library/nea-lgbtq-resources)

Open to ALL: Serving the GLBT Community in Your Library. (https://www.ala.org/rt/sites/ala.org.rt/files/content/professionaltools/160309-glbtrt-open-to-all-toolkit-online.pdf)

WPATH Standards of Care 8. (https://www.wpath.org/soc8)

Other Government Docs and Resources

Nondiscrimination on the Basis of Sex in Education Programs or Activities Receiving Federal Financial Assistance: Proposed Rule by the Education Department on July 12, 2022. (https://www.federalregister.gov/documents/2022/07/12/2022-13734/nondiscrimination-on-the-basis-of-sex-in-education-programs-or-activities-receiving-federal?utm_source=federalregister.gov&utm_medium=email&utm_campaign=subscription+mailing+list)

"Supporting LGBTQ Youth": Division of Adolescent and School Health (DASH), CDC. (https://www.cdc.gov/healthyyouth/safe-supportive-environments/lgbtq_youth.htm)

Transgender Student Policy and Procedure (RCW 28A.642.080): Washington State Legislature. (https://app.leg.wa.gov/rcw/default.aspx?cite=28A.642.080)

Resources for Students

GSA Court Victories: A Guide for LGBTQ High School Students, ACLU. (https://www.aclu.org/other/gsa-court-victories-guide-lgbtq-high-school-students)

Know Your Rights: Guide to the First Amendment for LGBTQ+ Youth in Delaware—ACLU of DE. (https://www.aclu-de.org/en/know-your-rights/kyr-guide-first-amendment-lgbtq-youth-delaware)

LGBTQ Students: Letters for When You're Fighting Discrimination, ACLU. (https://www.aclu.org/lgbtq-students-letters-when-youre-fighting-discrimination)

Rights & Activism, Learning for Justice. (https://www.learningforjustice.org/topics/rights-activism)

Youth Activism Project: "We train teens to become activist leaders in their communities." (https://www.youthactivismproject.org/)

Youth Organizing & GSA Resources, Illinois Safe Schools Alliance. (https://www.ilsafeschools.org/resources)

Appendix 2: Professional Development Provider Options

FOLLOWING ARE a few organizations that provide trans-focused professional development (PD) for educators. Also check out CenterLink: The Community of LGBTQ Centers (www.lgbtqcenters .org) for a comprehensive list of local and regional LGBTQ centers, many of which offer PD opportunities or resources.

A Queer Endeavor

A Queer Endeavor is a nationally recognized center for gender and sexual diversity in education. The organization builds partnerships with districts and school communities to create safer, more humanizing spaces in which LGBTQ+ youth, families, and staff can thrive. The work of A Queer Endeavor is made possible through our school and district partnerships, grants, and gifts, and the generous support of our community.

- A Queer Endeavor believes that schools and classrooms are places of possibility, where, as bell hooks says, "We have the opportunity to labor for freedom, to demand of our comrades, an openness of mind and heart that allows us to face reality even as we collectively imagine ways to move beyond boundaries, to transgress." This, hooks says, and A Queer Endeavor believes, is "education as the practice of freedom."

- A Queer Endeavor believes that centering the lived experiences, knowledge, and identities of students is essential for creating safe and humanizing classrooms.

- A Queer Endeavor believes in honoring teachers as professionals who want to do right by their students. To support teachers' processes of becoming, A Queer Endeavor creates access to professional learning that invites vulnerability, un/learning, accountability, and action.

- A Queer Endeavor believes that learning about identity, power, privilege, and oppression is tender work and A Queer Endeavor create "soft spaces of accountability" to support that deep learning.

- A Queer Endeavor believes that transformative justice in education relies on intersectional movement building and a commitment to collective liberation. This means recognizing that systems of oppression are intertwined. It means acknowledging that we all have issues of equity and justice that take us "out of [our] depth," as Charlene Carruthers says, and that we all have learning to do.

Better World Collaborative

Better World Collaborative (BWC) is a "social impact consultancy rooted in movement building and the creative arts. BWC understands that creating a better world requires working together and that, while no one can do everything, everyone can do something." BWC programming includes:

- Diversity, equity, and inclusion (DEI) workshops.
- Organizational growth and capacity-building.
- One-on-one leadership coaching and development.[1]

GLSEN

GLSEN Professional Development aims to empower educators to act in solidarity for LGBTQ students. Based on 25+ years of experience and research, GLSEN boasts a robust educator training program with a series of modules curated to cover an array of topics suitable for a diverse range of audiences.

GLSEN research shows that the presence of supportive educators can have a significant positive impact on LGBTQ students' academic achievement as well as on their psychological well-being and long-term educational aspirations. GLSEN Professional Development aims to empower educators to act in solidarity with LGBTQ students.

GLSEN's Professional Development Workshops will assist educators in building the following skills:

- Knowledge of LGBTQ student experiences in school.
- Understanding what solidarity can provide for LGBTQ students.
- Awareness of the prevalence of anti-LGBTQ language and behavior in schools.
- Willingness and ability to intervene when anti-LGBTQ name-calling and bullying occurs.
- Willingness and ability to utilize curriculum inclusive of LGBTQ people, history, and themes.
- Willingness to advocate for the rights of LGBTQ students and ensure safe schools for all.
- Access to resources and referral.

Note: For GLSEN Professional Development Workshops, the term *educator* includes, but is not limited to: current or future K–12 teachers, administrators, counselors, paraprofessionals, librarians, nurses, bus drivers, district staff, school resource officers, cafeteria workers, and so on.

The Human Rights Campaign's Welcoming Schools Program

HRC Foundation's Welcoming Schools is the most comprehensive bias-based bullying prevention program in the nation to provide LGBTQ+ and gender-inclusive professional development training, lesson plans, book lists, and resources specifically designed for educators and youth-serving professionals. The Welcoming Schools program uses an intersectional, anti-racist lens dedicated to actionable policies and practices. It uplifts school communities with critical tools to embrace family diversity, create LGBTQ+- and gender-inclusive schools, prevent bias-based bullying, and support transgender and non-binary students.

School-Based Training Options

When receiving professional development training from a Welcoming Schools Certified Facilitator, school leadership works in collaboration with the trainer to determine the prioritization of training modules based on individual school needs. Schools will be able to track their progress in creating a safer school climate by using the Welcoming Schools School Climate Assessment.

Teachers, school staff, and administrators will receive professional development and accompanying lesson plans, book lists, and practical tips on topics like:

- Preventing bias-based bullying in your school.
- Helping transgender and non-binary students to thrive.
- Creating classrooms that welcome all families.

District-Based Training Options

In addition to working with individual schools, the Welcoming Schools team works with districts to increase the internal capacity for districts to improve school climate by training facilitators within the district to deliver Welcoming Schools content to district educators

In a district-wide training, Welcoming Schools initially works with district leadership to select a cohort of in-district facilitators. These individuals are trained on site by Welcoming Schools staff during a four-day institute that equips them with the skills and tools to deliver Welcoming Schools professional development modules to elementary schools throughout their district.

Schools that complete each of the <u>Welcoming Schools modules</u> will have the opportunity to earn the <u>Seal of Excellence</u> by meeting benchmarks that support welcoming and safe schools.

Stonewall National Education Project (SNEP) Symposium

Stonewall National Education Project (SNEP), the education program of Stonewall National Museum & Archives, shares and implements strategies for LGBTQ-inclusive policies, inclusive practices, and curriculum through a national network of educators. As an advocate for the safety, inclusion, and value of LGBTQ students, SNEP focuses on centering the most vulnerable of LGBTQ students, with a focus on improving student achievement, attendance, and graduation rates.

Culminating in an annual three-day symposium that gathers more than 60 school districts from across the United States, school district administrators and board members, educators, and representatives from state departments of education, federal agencies, national and regional advocacy organizations, and community organizers doing work around LGBTQ+ youth are invited to attend.

Stonewall National Education Project also generates LGBTQ-inclusive curriculum and learning tools for high school environments that are available for purchase and distribution through grant-funded initiatives. Curriculum topics have included: LGBTQ-Inclusive Curriculum; The Day of Silence; Diversity: LGBT History Month and Beyond; Hispanic Heritage: Familia, Tradicíon, Música; and The Orlando 49: Documenting the Orlando Tragedy and Its Consequences.

The Trevor Project

The Trevor Project's mission is "to end suicide among lesbian, gay, bisexual, transgender, queer & questioning young people." The organization's five key programs include crisis services, peer support, research, public education, and advocacy. Specific trainings include Ally Training and CARE Training:

Ally Training

This training is designed to create dialogue around being an adult ally for LGBTQ youth by informing participants about common terminology, the "coming out" process, and challenges at home, in school, and in the community.

Through activities, participants are encouraged to explore their biases, build knowledge, and develop empathy. Participants will be able to:

- Describe various terminology within LGBTQ communities.
- Explain the unique challenges facing LGBTQ youth.
- Identify ways to create safer environments.
- Discuss the services offered by The Trevor Project.

CARE Training

The Trevor Project's CARE (Connect, Accept, Respond, Empower) Training is an interactive and intensive training that provides adults with an overview of suicide among lesbian, gay, bisexual, transgender, queer & questioning (LGBTQ) youth, and the different environmental stressors that contribute to the heightened risk for suicide.

After participating in this training, participants will be able to:

- Explain the risk factors and warning signs of suicide.
- Describe how to respond to a youth who is at risk for suicide and connect them to appropriate resources.

- Explain how to create supportive environments for all youth that promote resiliency and decrease the risk for suicide.
- Describe the services offered by The Trevor Project and how youth can access them.

YES Institute

YES Institute offers "communication and educational courses guided by leading research and a spirit of inquiry." The organization's commitment is "to create new ways for people to discover and view gender and orientation, while introducing a new context for people to relate to each other. Practical exercises grounded in theoretical presentations are a hallmark of YES Institute's work across all sectors of our community."

Specific YES Institute educational offerings include:

- Communication Solutions™.
- Communication Toolbox.
- Deciphering Gender & Orientation.
- A Communication Called "Bullying."
- Unconscious Bias in Learning Environments.
- Leadership in Action™.

National Education Association (NEA) Professional Learning on Safety, Bias, & LGTBQ+ Issues

The newly expanded LGBTQ+ Training Series is designed for all NEA members. With a focus on addressing bias around sexual orientation and gender identity, coupled with an intersectional focus on racial justice, this revised training series is full of the latest data, legal updates, and activities to empower members to support all students. This program covers six topic areas including supporting transgender students, exploring the intersections of race, and creating safer classrooms. Each training module is 2–3 hours in length and can be delivered in-person, virtually, or online via blended learning.

Topics

- Culturally Responsive Education
- Diversity & Inclusion
- Gender Equity
- LGBTQ+
- Positive School Environments
- Racial & Social Justice

Outcomes

- Learn how to create a safe school environment for students and staff
- Gain tools to address bias around sexual orientation and gender identity

---

Note

1. Full disclosure: co-author Rebecca Kling is also a cofounder of BWC.

Appendix 3: Guidance Template for Classroom Libraries

This example guidance was provided by educator Jessica Cisneros.

BOOK	*Pink Is for Boys* written by Robb Pearlman and illustrated by Eda Kaban
GRADE	Preschool and kindergarten
TOPICS	Gender stereotypes
KEY VOCAB	*Stereotype*
DISCUSSION PROMPTS	Can a color be only for certain kinds of people? Why do you think people sometimes have stereotypes? Have you ever heard of a different stereotype before? Why can a stereotype be a problem?

(Continued)

(*Continued*)

ADDITIONAL SUGGESTIONS	Emphasize the qualifier of *some*: instead of saying, for example, "Girls like pink," say, "*Some* girls like pink." Instead of "Boys like sports," say, "*Some* boys like sports." This can be emphasized by having students say statements like this themselves. Using the book *Pink Is for Boys* as inspiration, students can write their own "_____ is for girls" and/or "_____ is for boys" page, or color a pre-written page.
BE PREPARED FOR. . .	If some students in your class are already holding tight to stereotypes about colors and gender, you may need to revisit with them individually.

Index

Page numbers followed by *f* refer to figures.